Write with Flash
Memoir, Biography, Fact and Fiction

Dr Stephen Mark Richards

Illustrations: (Margaret) Joyce Richards

Cover Design: S.M. Richards 2015; Subject: The Kelpies by Andy Scott, Falkirk, Scotland.

First Edition: Published UK: August 2015

Second Edition: Published UK: September 2017

Published in UK English, United Kingdom

Ampurlife Books in conjunction with LuLu

Second Edition: Published UK: September 2017

ISBN: 978-0-244-33386-7

Ampurlife Books - Ampurlife.com

4 Lake View, St John, PL11 3AW, United Kingdom

Write with Flash

Memoir, Biography, Fact and Fiction

Books by Stephen Mark Richards

Find out more at the end of this book.

Tornado Spring

This is the true story of a journey through the full height of the United States during the worst tornado outbreak on record.

Wild Summer

We travelled west through the Rocky Mountains to the Pacific Ocean, up through Canada's Cascade Mountains and then south, through the giant coastal redwood forests, to San Francisco.

Desert Winter

It is an adventure of a life-time, from the Pacific to the Atlantic, traversing the deserts of the southern United States.

Conquering America

The trilogy of Tornado Spring, Wild Summer and Desert Winter in one complete volume.

Florida without Disney

How can a visitor to Florida embark on an amazing journey through time and space?

Write with Flash

Discover the secrets of storytelling and perhaps you will soon be sharing your unique story.

Short Shorts and Shorts: Volume 1

The first volume in a series of short story books fully illustrated by Joyce. Unsuitable for young children.

Holly Marie and the Small Tall Tree

Holly Marie explored the world of observation with her friend Rabbit. For children 2 to 6 years.

Contents continued overleaf ...

Contents continued ....

1. Write with Flash

Flash is a writing form that can help aspiring writers to become published authors and Write with Flash aims to show how that can be achieved.

There is often a focus on developing all aspects of the child, and rightly so. However, that does not mean we should forget adults, who may have slipped through childhood without anyone noticing the possibilities hidden away inside them. Let us face it; few people can aspire to be great writers, or great at anything else for that matter. However, it is not all about being great.

Our aspirations are about unlocking the potential that each of us has inside. This is further enhanced when we are able to help each other to flourish in ways that we may never have realised were possible. Yes, children are special, but adults are too. Just because someone was unable to reach their potential, it does not mean that they should be consigned to a heap. For most people, it is not too late to chase their ambitions for personal growth and fulfillment

Generally, most people fall short of reaching their true potential and some of those people will wish to address that fact. This is worthwhile, even when our only desire is to prove to ourselves that we have hidden talents that we are able to develop and exploit. It all comes back to being the best we can.

Naturally, it is important to help children to tap and develop their potential. In that way, they are less likely to go through life feeling that they could have been so much more. However, that focus on children does not mean that we, either as individuals or as a society, should neglect the untapped potential of adults. We all have untapped potential and we can all experience the joy arising from developing our talents.

Many people have written books but their number pales into insignificance when compared to the number of people who would like to write a book and never do. This does not mean that those unwritten books would have been without merit had they been written. On the contrary, what it really means is that millions of fascinating stories go to the grave with their would-be creators. The sad fact is, the unique qualities that each of those potential creators would have brought to those untold stories, were never shared.

Everyone has stories, many have the desire to share those stories, but relatively few people have the determination to turn dreams into reality. The message to all aspiring writers is to stop aspiring and start writing. Without doubt, there are more unnoticed people with the potential to shine than are ever discovered. Only by sharing your light can anyone see how uniquely your light shines.

1.1 Background

Write with Flash emerged from the idea that many writing techniques, that are primarily applied to the writing of fictional works, are equally applicable to both fact-based and fictional stories. This book takes the short story format called flash fiction and identifies ways in which it may be used for writing practise, scene development and honing the writer's analytical skills. Write with Flash also shows how the writing form called flash fiction can easily be adapted and used to write, analyse and develop true stories such as memoirs and biographies.

Much of the knowledge contained within this book is used by most writers of fictional works. However here, that knowledge is used to assist writers who are aspiring to write either fiction or fact-based works. People seeking to improve their writing are shown how the flash fiction format can be used to improve their written storytelling. Write with Flash uniquely shows how many of the problems that face the writer of fiction also face those wishing to recount major life events.

Flash fiction, a word limited story format, is proposed as a tool for practising the development of both writing and analytical skills. The name, flash fiction, may lead some to believe, erroneously, that this writing form is only applicable to fictional subject matter. Throughout, it is shown that the flash format can be used to practise writing and develop scenes for fact-based stories. Write with Flash is intended to show you a way to rapidly develop your writing and analytical skills regardless of your writing ambitions.

My background is far from unique but it does provide a useful platform from which to write a book of this kind. Since 'Write with Flash' is aimed at aspiring writers, then it must be supportive of the efforts of those starting-out writers as they aim to develop themselves. Delivering such a tall order relies on delivering accessible and usable information. It is hoped that this will produce a pleasurable and exciting experience for aspiring writers and help them to learn the new skills they need.

I have drawn upon my experience and knowledge as both an educator and a factual writer. This has not only been a fulfilling work but also tremendously exciting and a lot of fun. Skills in fictional writing, exploited by the best fiction writers, have been developed over many years of practise. This means that much of their knowledge has become second nature to them, almost instinctual. Naturally, such writers direct most of their energy to their craft and much can be learned by examining the work of such writers. At the same time, aspiring writers need to consider and develop their own writing skills. Most are not aiming to become great writers. Ambitions are often far more humble. Many people just want to be able to write a book which readers will enjoy. If they can achieve that, then they have achieved everything.

When it comes to learning how to write, it is useful to learn how to be consciously aware of your critical and analytical skills. This is achieved through active practise. Throughout this book, aspiring writers are encouraged to practise their analytical skills and through this, it is hoped that we can all raise our awareness of why we have the reactions that we do to the various stories that we encounter.

My background in education also means that my approach to writing this book involves reading what other writers have to say on the subject. I say this because I want to make another important point. No artist should ever worry that studying how other artists approach problems will pervert their own personal style. Of course, people are excellent mimics, but people are also fundamentally creative. All trained artists study other artists and literary artists are no different. Even if you have not undertaken formal training in fiction writing, in fact, especially if you have not undertaken formal training, a fundamental part of your self-education must be the study of other writers and the techniques that they employ.

1.2 Aims of Write with Flash

You can't allow what other people think of you hamper, or even stop you. For example, if you want to learn to play golf, there is no substitute to taking yourself out to the nearest public golf course. Of course, you can mess about in your garden, hidden from the eyes of the world but, at the end of the day, you are not going to learn to play golf. You must be willing to allow others to watch your progress.

Somehow, there seems to be an assumption that writing is different, perhaps because it seems quite easy to hide away in your writing room. It is not different. Both are skill-based activities which are developed and practised in a public space. If you wish to progress then you still need to get out there where people can see what you're doing. You need to share your writing with others and you need to hear any criticisms that they have the courage to tell you. It is not always appreciated that giving criticism can take courage because, even when it is constructive, it can still offend.

Obviously, you will hope that the more experienced golfer (in our analogy) will have a quiet word in your ear explaining how you might improve. However, you can neither demand nor expect this. There will always be someone who is sufficiently arrogant to shout at you across the golf course.

"You stink. Get a move on or get off."

Ignore them. If their idea of constructive criticism is the destruction of a person's embryonic confidence, then it is they who are in the greatest need of personal improvement, not you.

From this it follows, that if you are frightened to begin to consider yourself a writer then you shouldn't be. Writing should be inclusive. This means that you have taken your first step on the road to becoming a writer as soon as you write your first sentence. We all have the same struggles. We all have a desire to communicate ideas, information or emotions in such a way that the words on the paper capture the thoughts in our heads. Writing can be a wonderful way to communicate both to ourselves and to others. No one knows it all. We are all learners to some degree and no matter who you are, you have every right to engage with others through your written communication.

Of the many people who believe they have a book in them, some also aspire to get that book out. What these people often lack is the training to allow them to fulfill their ambitions. This is equally true of those desiring to write their first novel, as it is of those who believe that they have a memoir or biographical story that should be made available to a wider audience.

For many, there are reasons why formal education in writing is not a realistic option. Such writers are left to educate themselves on writing craft. I have read many books purporting to assist the aspiring writer to create their first work. Without doubt, much of the advice contained within these books can be helpful if the reader is able to formulate their own methods of extracting the points that are pertinent to them, their situation, and their genre. This is extremely difficult to achieve when first starting out because utilizing the information appropriately requires a certain degree of pre-knowledge. As a result, it is naive to think that your knowledge can be fully formed after reading a single book on a particular subject. You may not wish to hear this, but the reality is that knowledge only becomes understanding through active processing.

I must admit, a good part of the reason that I wanted to write this particular book was to actively process my own learning to date. My background in teaching, instruction and assessment for people with very special needs, through to graduate, post-graduate and doctoral levels of education, has taught me many important lessons. One of these lessons is appreciating the fact that there is no better way to really learn something than to go out and teach others about it. You do not need to be the most knowledgeable person in the world on the particular subject. You just need to have some knowledge, understanding or experience, which is of value to your audience, and this can be true at every level of the learning process.

Writing this book is, for me, working to make myself a better writer. For you, if you want to make the most out of Write with Flash, you need to explain to your friends and family all the things that you learn here. In that way, you will consolidate and organise your learning in a way that you would probably never have believed was possible.

Write with Flash details a method aimed at allowing you to develop your own story telling skills. As an aspiring writer, you can practise and rapidly hone your writing skills using the flash fiction format. You can also rapidly develop your critical assessment skills and use them to analyse works by other writers. Try not to limit your critical assessment to books alone. Remember, stories exist in many forms and you can use your learning to analyse film and theatre too. In the end, you should have aquired the tools that you need to critically assess your own work and this is perhaps the most important key to creating a work to share with a wider audience.

I also wish to encourage a joy in writing creatively. Enjoyment is a strange emotion. We can enjoy even the most difficult tasks if we are satisfied that we have met our objectives. It is particularly important to anyone starting out with creative writing to identify the joy they feel from engaging in their writing. Whenever a writer, regardless of their levels of ability and experience, shares their work, they are also sharing their joy of creative writing.

When you have finished reading Write with Flash, there is one important question you should ask yourself. Has Write with Flash been helpful to you as an aspiring writer? If you are able to answer that question in the affirmative then you will have definitely made progress towards fulfilling your writing ambitions.

1.3 What is a story?

Although sometimes erroneously attributed to Mark Twain, and to me sounding thoroughly Dickensian, the quotation: "nothing is certain but death and taxes" is known to have originated in a 1789 letter written by one of the Founding Fathers of the United States, Benjamin Franklin. However, speaking more universally, nothing is certain but change.

Many years ago I suffered a major depression and from that experience I came to realise that the only sure thing in life is change. I used that idea to give me the hope I needed to climb up out of that dark place. Thereafter, whenever I try to understand my life, just as many people are prone to try to understand theirs on occasion, the only answer that I can formulate is that a lifetime is a container for change.

Each life contains its own unique set of changes. When people believe that they have a unique story to tell, they are, without doubt, correct in that assertion. A story too is a container for change. This link between life and story is at the heart of both memoirs and fictions. Both factual and fictional accounts aim to show how events, actions and reactions, shape changes in the central characters contained within, whether they are real people or something invented by the mind of a writer. In both cases, the one inevitability is change.

1.4 Writers' groups

Writers' groups are a great way to become involved in creative writing. Usually, they consist of a small group of people who meet just for the pleasure of writing. Groups often make no claims to expertise but this is a benefit rather than a drawback. What people in these groups share is their love of creative writing. Each person has his or her own individual style, philosophy and preferences. Each produces unique stories.

Crucially, each member has a desire to be creative and to support others who also wish to write and share the product of their creativity.

I first joined a writer's group in order to engage with others who enjoy writing fiction. I could not have anticipated the benefits. I discovered much about my own writing voice and myself. Right from the very outset, group membership helped me to develop my fiction writing skills. Group members provide a ready-made audience of fellow writers where we can all experiment with new techniques. Many writers talk about writing as a solitary activity and in many cases, it is. However, being part of a writer's group can help the aspiring writer to feel less isolated.

There is only one real condition to joining a writing group. You must fully engage with the group and openly share your ideas. It is not just about how a writing group supports you. It is, equally, about how you reciprocate as a group member. If you can do this then your experiences of writing groups will surely make you feel less isolated in your writing endeavours.

1.5 Accessibility and dyslexia

The readability of books, and in particular educational books, is extremely important. However, many people have difficulties accessing books due to presentation issues rather than the material they contain. For instance, over 10% of people suffer from dyslexia, a significant issue affecting an individual's ability to read. Research has provided information about the issues affecting readability and identified techniques that improve the presentation of printed material.

This book aims to encourage and help people to become more involved in writing. It targets a broad audience regardless of the issues that provide barriers to their progress. As a result, readability is a specific issue considered when formatting this book. There are two types of written work in this book: firstly, knowledge; and secondly, stories. Each type of material presents its own specific demands and so some differences exist in their presentation. Admittedly, I do not have full control over presentation and so the edition, which you are reading now, may not fully adhere to the following standards, as I would have liked.

Research shows that readers can be assisted by text justified at the left margin only, meaning that lines of text are of different lengths. Left margin justification results in an uneven, or ragged, right margin, which is more readable for all readers, and specifically beneficial to dyslexic readers. Fully justified text, a common standard in printed books, increases the prevalence of wandering white 'rivers' flowing down the page. These are created by the adjusted white spaces between words necessitated by forcing the words to form a straight line at both the left and right margins. These rivers are particularly distracting for dyslexic readers who further struggle with hyphenated splits in words at the end of lines. Hyphenated splits are another common consequence of fully justified text.

Rivers also become more prevalent by the use of double spaces to separate sentences. This is a technique often found in documents created by traditional manual typists. It was thought that a larger separation between sentences would aid readability but this is no longer thought to be the case. Consequently, this book uses single spaces between sentences.

In modern word-processing and printing, a publisher often has the choice of a wide variety of character shapes or styles, generally referred to as text fonts. Perhaps, there is often a natural tendency to try to make the words on the page look pretty by adding small embellishments, called serifs, to each alphanumeric character. However, the impacts of serifs on readability are complex.

Although the results of research can be inconsistent, it does seem to suggest that serifs significantly aid the readability of print for most readers. Unfortunately, serifs also appear to reduce readability for dyslexic readers. When it comes to presenting text on-screen, fonts without serifs often prove best for all readers. As a result, it is probably best to use fonts with serifs for printed books and fonts without serifs for books when read on-screen, such as Kindle editions.

Dyslexic readers are also aided by short, clearly defined paragraphs, which are marked by indenting the first word and adding a line space between paragraphs. Implementation is straightforward when material occurs in paragraph format. It is less appropriate for stories that include a large amount of dialogue. Small indents and the removal of line spaces between paragraphs are preferable for dialogue as they reduce the number of orphans (words that appear disconnected from the rest of the text). For these reasons, the formatting of stories should use smaller indents and less line spacing than informative books.

Problems also arise for dyslexic readers from the use of all capital letters (used sometimes to denote shouting), underlining (used for emphasis), or italisising (often used to indicate thoughts). Although such presentation styles cause difficulties for dyslexic readers, they still commonly exist in published works. However, such formatting techniques become unnecessary through careful use of narrative, or through speech, thought and action tags.

2. Past, Present and Future

If you just want to read some stories right now then jump straight to 'Quick Fix Flash' where you will find some examples of flash fictions. Don't forget to return here to find out more about flash fiction. In particular, take some time to study the Toolkit, as this will help you to get the most from the stories in this book and should prove a valuable starting point when endeavoring to write your own stories.

2.1 What is flash?

Flash fiction is fast becoming the de-facto name for a range of short story formats. To quote Pamelyn Casto:

> 'Other names for it include short-short stories, sudden, postcard, minute, furious, fast, quick, skinny, and micro fiction. In France such works are called nouvelles. In China this type of writing has several interesting names: little short story, pocket-size story, minute-long story, palm-sized story, and my personal favorite, the smoke-long story (just long enough to read while smoking a cigarette).'

Quotation from:

Flashes On The Meridian: Dazzled by Flash Fiction by Pamelyn Casto, 2002

However, trying to tie down an agreed definition of flash fiction based upon size is impossible except that, in all definitions, the word count is almost always below 2000 words. In fact, most proponents of this art form are in agreement upon word counts between 300 and 1000 words. Even this stipulation is far from definitive as many writers of super short stories aim for story lengths under 300 words, or even less than 100. There are even special short story forms such as a drabble (a name originating from a sketch in Monty Python's Big Red Book) at around 100 words and 55 Fiction, which is a form limited to a maximum of 55 words, or a requirement of exactly 55 words. Both of those forms would also undoubtedly qualify as flash fiction.

2.2 Six little words

Regardless of the length of a short story, a flash fiction should still be a story. To illustrate this point we can look at a now famous six word story, often dubiously attributed to Ernest Hemingway. The story goes like this:

For sale: Baby shoes, never worn.

This is an extreme type of flash fiction which produced a large number of followers of this specific format. If you allow yourself to feel the 'For sale: Baby shoes, never worn' story then an entire story world emerges. I would not want to pre-determine your feelings or the untold story which emerged for you but it is almost certainly true that for most people the story is quite sad.

However, this example also reveals another important aspect of the relationship between writer and reader. The story does not need to be sad. The reader has complete freedom to bring their own experiences and interpretations to the reading experience and this is their right. They own their reading experience and the writer is powerless to determine that experience. As a writer, you may be aiming to invoke certain emotions but we should equally welcome our reader's individuality.

Such multiple interpretations are supported by the history of the 'Baby Shoes' story. In 1910, some years prior to Ernest Hemmingway becoming a writer, a newspaper headline 'Tragedy of Baby's Death is Revealed in Sale of Clothes' appeared in the Spokane Press. Then, in 1917, William R. Kane wrote a piece in a periodical, The Journal of Information for Literary Workers, where he described an idea of a grief-stricken woman who had lost her baby and suggested the title of 'Little Shoes, Never Worn'. By 1921, the story had been given an alternate 'happy' interpretation when, in an issue of the satirical magazine, Judge, a baby carriage (or pram) was used instead of shoes. The buyer offers condolences only to be informed that the sale was due to the happy news of the birth of twins.

It was not until 1991 that the story was first connected to Hemmingway in a book, by the writer Peter Miller, called Get Published! Get Produced!: A Literary Agent's Tips on How to Sell Your Writing. This was in fact 30 years after Hemmingway's death. Regardless, the attribution seems to have stuck and Hemmingway is often cited as the originator.

2.3 Changes

This story, which is perhaps the most commonly told tale about the history of flash fiction, illustrates that even well-renowned modern writers have been linked with the form. When we consider traditional short stories we find that flash fiction has had an even longer history. Many examples of myths and ghost stories, epistles and parables, fables and fairy tales fall very easily into the flash fiction category. However, the rapid increase in online and self-publishing has helped flash fiction gain an enormous global following. It is now a popular writing format from the Americas to China and all points between. This growth has led flash fiction to become increasingly accepted as a valuable literary form resulting in a tremendous growth in the number of works now considered prestigious.

I remember an occasion a few years ago, when I emailed a text to my stepson who, luckily for me, happens to be a journalist and editor. After a day I messaged him again to ask what he thought of it. His answer came as a valuable lesson. He simply sent back 'TLDR' which I eventually discovered meant 'too long, didn't read'. I had failed to grab his attention in the first sentence. He had then looked at the size of the document and simply put it to one side.

I realised that a new breed of reader had emerged. These readers grew up in the social media age, where messages are often delivered in punch-lines, slogans, phrases or just a couple of sentences. People are no longer so ready to read unbroken blocks of text. Some of the 'old school' may claim that this has encouraged short attention spans, whereas, those who have embraced social media often feel that they have developed the skills of directness and brevity. They rely on the intelligence of the reader to complete the missing parts thus avoiding over-explanation. Flash fiction is ideally suited to this modern 'social media' approach to communication.

In addition, the growth of social media, blogging and internet publishing, has provided an accessible forum for both readers and writers of flash fiction. Contrary to popular belief, social media is almost entirely composed of fiction. I am uncertain if this constitutes a problem but many people believe it to be factual and it is through such routes that stories, such as the one previously mentioned regarding Ernest Hemmingway, spread to become part of a global reality. Social media is almost entirely flash fiction in a mass, and less crafted, form.

There appears to be a feeling that the modern world and modern life has a much faster pace than it had a couple of decades ago. If this is true, then flash fiction probably feels more 'in tune' with the modern world. Small pieces are so much easier when being read on-screen and this is even more important when reading from extremely small mobile phone screens. More people now have almost their entire reading experience on their mobile phone and this experience is facilitated by presenting text in extremely small chucks.

2.4 Flash now

If we wish to communicate with the widest possible audience then it is no longer sufficient to limit our consideration of how we deliver our prose to using traditional paper forms, computer screens, tablets, and e-book readers. It may be that more writers will embrace delivery through mobile phone screens and use super small flash fiction, not only as a work in its own right, but also to deliver prequels to encourage readers to move from their mobile phones to delivery platforms which are more suited to larger works.

Some may argue that a synopsis or elevator pitch is akin to such a prequel, but I believe that true flash prequels would be separate stories in their own right. They would require all the same skill and care that is given to more substantial works and they would exist to drive the modern short piece reader to full-scale novels. For me, regardless of the pace of life, there will always be a place for more substantial literary works.

Whatever ways writers bend flash fiction to meet their own objectives, readers need quality. Brevity is not an excuse for inattention to detail. Writers need to be just as conscious of their writing craft. However, for those wishing to start writing stories, whether it is to begin to develop the skills to produce longer works, or for those engaged in writing stories for fun, flash fiction provides a highly adaptable literary form. Although it is difficult to write flash fiction which excels, it is relatively easy for a novice writer to create a finished piece using the flash fiction format. For someone learning the craft, it is certainly less daunting than trying to write a full-length novel or memoir. Psychologically speaking, regardless of the size of a work, finishing a piece can be tremendously encouraging and rewarding.

In addition, even established writers can use flash fiction to build more substantial works. This idea is not universally accepted because it can create problems with a lack of connective material. In other words, it can become difficult to draw the short pieces into a single cohesive work. However, flash fiction does have a number of uses for writers of more substantial works and I believe that many writers use flash fiction as a technique, even if they may not always recognise the fact.

Amongst other uses, flash fiction can be used to: create scenes; develop dialogue; produce cliff hangers; explore semantics; break writer's block; and generate fresh ideas. Writers can practise the creation of situations which are meaningful in their own right. This does not mean that the writer ignores the context of the story as a whole. After all, even at the very start of any story a context exists of which the reader is unaware. The context which exists in the writer's mind still informs that opening scene.

In this chapter I have tried to give some flavour of the history, variety and application of the flash fiction form. In addition, I have attempted to provide some insight into my own thoughts and feelings on how this literary form can be used for everyone, from the novice writer to those who are widely published, but still consider themselves to be learners.

For me, we are all learners and hopefully we will never stop learning. Crucially, as people who write, we should enjoy the process. What is this craft if we are not excited by it, if we do not enjoy it, if we do not share it, if we are not inclusive, and if we do not value every writer's best efforts? Those qualities of our writing experiences are, by far, the most important.

3. Toolkit

One of the problems for writers, who are just starting out, is that they often attempt to write a book sized work without undertaking sufficient training and self-education. Writers are always trying to improve and, since you are reading this, it is probable that you too are working to improve your knowledge and skills. In this section, you will find a range of issues described and discussed which are relevant to storytelling. Unlike many other sources, this toolkit is equally applicable to both fictional work and fact-based work such as memoirs and biographies.

To gain maximum benefit from a book it is important to process its contents. This means using the information rather than simply reading it. In writing this book, I am required to process and organise my prior learning and such active processing is highly beneficial. Through active learning, we can all improve the stories that we have been struggling to tell. In addition, we can also achieve a greater understanding of why and how our stories have improved. This allows us to make major steps forward in our development as writers.

At various points in Write with Flash, you will encounter suggested activities to facilitate the active processing of the information in this chapter. Even if you decide to ignore such activities, it is still useful to think about the ideas discussed in this section whilst you are reading the Quick Fix Flash stories included in the book. Most readers should find that engaging in such a process will produce a more detailed understanding of the works of others, even if such an improved appreciation is, at first, relatively vague. This helps to develop further the necessary analytical skills.

Each section in this chapter is designed to stand alone, as far as possible, for the purposes of using these sections as discrete tools. As a result, if you wish to revise a single section, there should be no need to revise the entire chapter. In addition, some ideas are relevant within several different contexts. This means tackling certain issues within several sections but from different angles. For example, the way we develop our characters is relevant to several of the tools discussed in this chapter. As a result, character is one of several issues addressed in more than one section.

More experienced writers too can benefit from the approach outlined here. Flash can be used as a vehicle to develop both fictional and fact-based works. Experienced fiction writers will no doubt have encountered the types of suggestions outlined here in their previous learning experiences but should still find the ideas expressed in this chapter useful.

However, Write with Flash is primarily aimed at writers who are less experienced. For some of those writers this will be their first training. Other writers, particularly those who have studied many other books on writing craft, may welcome an explicit reminder of the processes and techniques that they may already employ, even if, at a subconscious level.

Many of the ideas expressed here are generally applicable to fiction writing and some variation or combination of them can be found in any number of books aimed at helping the learning writer to produce better fiction. Guidelines also form a key part of most creative writing courses. Naturally, each set of guidelines is different. The novel approach in here is the tailoring of guidelines around the use of the flash format to provide a vehicle for the development of both fictional and fact-based works.

Try not to think of these guidelines as rules, even though you may find similar information presented as such in some publications. It is far better to think of this as a toolkit of suggestions. These guidelines are pointers to ways of working that you may not have already considered. You can practise applying these suggestions to see how well they work for you. If something does not fit with what you wish to achieve with your writing then there is no need to use that particular suggestion.

26

Individual style, what some people call 'finding your voice' is important. Nobody wants a world where we all follow the same route and writing styles become more homogenous. Nevertheless, some writers may discover a type of liberation in their writing by using the suggestions presented in this toolkit.

3.1 Imagination

Some people have strange and erroneous beliefs regarding imagination and creativity. Many people would immediately associate the creation of fine art paintings and drawings, the composition of musical scores and the writing of fictional books as being creative and therefore requiring imagination. Far fewer people accept the idea that looking at a painting, playing from a musical score or reading a book are creative activities. However, the act of appreciating, interpreting and experiencing the creative output of others is itself a creative process.

Creativity and imagination extends well beyond the excepted world of the arts. The scientist or natural philosopher, who imagines the composition of reality and creates ways of investigating and interpreting their speculations, is every bit as creative as an impressionist artist. Even choosing a plant for the garden is creative. So it is important that we should not be too elitist about who is, and who is not, creative. We fail to recognise the imaginative and creative product of others only when we, as individuals, fail to adequately engage our own imaginations.

Even in the accepted world of the arts, people can sometimes fail to appreciate the creative and imaginative aspects of others. This seems to be particularly true of modern art forms. Failure to appreciate the creative output of others can lead to elitist thinking with regard to those art works. For example, you may hear people opining that modern art is not art. Such elitism is a danger to your own creativity and imagination. How can you expect others to take the time to truly experience your creative output if you are unwilling to afford that respect to the creative output of others?

If you write creatively then you are an artist. You must use your imagination regardless of the genre in which you write. Fact-based works require no less imagination. Events must be interpreted, motivations surmised and stories created. In the world of any human endeavour, the sciences, the arts, or even everyday tasks, creativity and imagination are the tools we need to be enlightened. As a result, it is imperative for any writer, regardless of the genre in which they write, to practise and hone their imaginative and creative skills. Without imagination there is no story, not even in science. Without story there is no meaning.

The introduction of a theme, a moral or a philosophy, into a story also requires creativity and imagination. For example, the theme that 'love conquers all' is not self evident from events. If you, as a writer, wish your audience to interpret story events as producing the conclusion that love conquers all then you need to craft those events such that they deliver such a conclusion. The writer needs to imagine how events can be linked to show the theme or philosophy and then deliver those links to the reader.

Even when writing a fact-based story such as a memoir, a theme can be extremely important. It can provide significance to events which, although meaningful to the person who experienced the events, may fail to be meaningful to others. It is the writer's responsibility to embed the content that will make their story, fact or fiction, meaningful to a wider audience.

When specifically writing fiction, for me, the key is to make sure that it is fiction that I am writing. This can be a problem, particularly for those making their first attempts at fictional writing. It is so easy to end up with too many elements of oneself inhabiting the characters. This tends to result in quite flat characters because of the tendency to portray ourselves only in a way that we find acceptable to our own psychological well-being. Recreating self-deluded images of ourselves lacks both imagination and creativity.

Neither is it a good idea to base our characters on people we know: friends; family; neighbours; or even worse, enemies. Again, the tendency will be to limit the emotional and behavioural world of such characters. As a result, they will fail to fascinate or surprise us as writers and they are likely to have exactly the same impact on our readers.

Even if we believe that we are able to liberate these known people by imbuing them with some fictional characteristics, such characterizations are still likely to be shallow. From a creative point of view, the greatest problem is the resulting lack of imagination and creativity.

Naturally, we do need to use personal experience to inform our characters but this is not the same as copying our characters from that experience. Characters need to be built, with lives, histories, personalities, problems, limitations, emotions etc. These characters then need to encounter situations or events and only then do we draw on our personal experience to work out the characters reactions to, and interpretations of, those situations and events.

For any writer, it can be a truly liberating experience to try to make your main characters as far removed from yourself, and the people best known to you, as possible. For example: you can start with a main character with a different gender to yourself; perhaps another could come from a different ethnic background; hold different religious beliefs; or even be a different species. Writers of science fiction are well accustomed to placing themselves in the minds of aliens, monsters and superheroes. You can even place yourself within what would normally be an inanimate object. In fiction, there is absolutely no reason why the pot cannot talk to the kettle, that the moon cannot be angry with the earth, or that the sea cannot fall in love with the sky.

Flash fiction is the perfect writing form for practising with your imagination. It can be used to quickly move your mind in and out of truly invented characters inhabiting invented worlds. You can practise putting yourself inside the fictional being and imagine. What would they think, feel, or do in this situation? This is true even when the 'fictional being' is yourself in your own memoir. Your conscious recollection of events may not be reflective of the real truth. Such truth may be buried in alternative reconstructions of events which await discovery somewhere deep in your imagination.

3.2 Tension and conflict

There can be a tendency for those starting to write fiction to start at the beginning. By this, I mean you as the writer seek to develop your main characters. You want the reader to know your main characters, know what makes them tick, know how they arrived at this point, and understand why the situation is so difficult for them. You want the reader to empathise with your characters. When the characters suffer conflict you want the reader to understand how they must feel when confronted by each situation that they encounter. The difficulty is; how can we build this understanding without first providing at least some back story to explain what makes the characters react and behave in the ways they do?

I have read many books on the art and craft of writing fiction. Many of these books give a simple rule on how to start a story and that rule is, start with conflict. Before outlining what this means, I want to say that I don't entirely agree with this rule. Nevertheless, understanding this rule does help us to create captivating beginnings and, if we fail to captivate our readers from the very first, then many readers will not read any further.

The problem arises when we try to deliver too much information to the reader before the action starts. To avoid this, it has been commonly proposed that a story should dive straight into the main conflict. This is the conflict which drives our plot. It is the main purpose of the story and it forms the grounds on which all key battles are fought.

If you do chose to follow this method of starting a longer story then you are actually attempting to avoid explaining the context of your story. In other words, you do not try to explain any events leading up to the current conflict. That is all considered back-story. Although the writer must know and understand the full back-story, it is not necessary for the reader to know it all. Any important aspects of back-story can be told later, once the reader has become totally engaged.

Some advice to starting writers even suggests writing the story and then throwing away the first chapter, or even the first few chapters. In other words, it is suggested that you discard all the parts prior to the start of the main conflict. The problem with this approach, as I see it, is that even if the conflict is exciting, the reader will have tremendous difficulty having any empathy with the characters involved.

This leaves us with a dilemma. On the one hand, we risk boring the reader if we start out by introducing the characters. On the other hand, , if we try to start out by introducing the main conflict, we risk readers lacking empathy for the characters. There is, however, a third way. If we introduce tension first, then we are able to show who our characters are without telling the reader their back stories. Tension arises from difficult situations through which we can come to see and understand the feelings, motives, morals and behaviours of the central characters.

Introducing characters through their interaction with tense situations allows the development of empathy, so that when they are subjected to the main conflict of the story, our readers already care about them. This strategy provides the means of introducing our characters without losing the audience. Information is slipped to the reader through the back door by seeing how the character deals with the tension that the writer has created. In fact, this is the strategy of many successful novelists.

Tension can often hold the key to opening your story, rather than conflict, regardless of whether your story is fact-based or purely fictional. If you start with tension then you have a good chance of captivating your reader and making them care for your characters. Once your readers care, they will be far more forgiving. You are then in the perfect position to introduce the central conflict of your piece and your reader will care how your characters feel. They will empathise with them. You will have successfully invoked an emotional reaction in the reader and it is those emotions which will carry your reader all the way to the end of your story. It is this empathy which will allow you to develop your characters more fully later in the story.

I recently read again the start of the Life of Pi by Yann Martel. The author creates tension through the characters relationships with the other pupils in his school, a beautiful girl, and Pi's relationships with his immediate family members. These are not elements of the main plot or the central conflict but they allow the reader to know Pi through the way he approaches these tensions in his life.

Martel also slips in the theme of Pi's attempts to understand good and evil, and his relationship with God. This theme then runs through the entire story and informs the central conflict of the story. In that central conflict, Pi allows the dark side of his character to emerge and dominate his normally dominant social self in order to survive. Minor tensions preceding the survival situation allow the reader to know Pi's social self and start to build empathy with him. The theme allows the central conflict to develop on moral and philosophical lines, rather than only within the physical and emotional dimensions.

Life of Pi is a full scale novel and Yann Martel has sufficient time and space to develop all these aspects of his story.

In flash writing, however, we do not have such luxury. Nevertheless, it is important to deliver the key features that we have just discussed. As writers, we need to focus on developing empathy for our characters through their interactions with tension and conflict. We can still aspire to use the same basic structure in flash fiction even if we rely even more heavily on the reader to imagine what the back stories could be.

The general aim should be to start in tension, work through conflict, then guide to resolution.

Tension is not simply the act of placing obstacles before your characters. Obstacles must be real and threatening in order to create tension. Obstacles form mini stories in themselves. Such stories are often referred to as sub-plots and need to be crafted with almost as much care as the main plot. An obstacle serves no purpose if it is simply there to cause trouble. An obstacle allows the writer to develop the character's back-story – who they are and what makes them who they are. It is through the character's reactions and struggles with obstacles that we will build our empathy with these characters for the time when they face the true trials that lie ahead.

It might be useful, at this point, to distinguish more fully between tension and conflict especially when it comes to dealing with the principle source of conflict within a story. Many fights are fought throughout any book, irrespective of whether the story is fact-based or purely fictional. Some of these fights are really skirmishes and relate to the sub-plots which create tension. Other fights are battles, driven by the central conflict, and are part of the primary story formed from the main plot.

As previously discussed, tension can be seen as a special type of conflict that is relevant to the main story because it helps to develop our characters and our reader's empathy with them. On the other hand, the central conflict provides the underlying energy which drives our entire story. Tension informs our understanding of the characters in terms of their values, emotions and behaviours whilst the central conflict is directly related to the underlying values which guide and direct the main story. Tension drives our sub-plots whereas conflict drives our plot. It is only the central conflict which has the power to completely overwhelm our lead character and endanger them to such an extent that they may lose everything, perhaps their lives, or more dramatically, perhaps even their souls.

It is possible to become confused when first starting to delineate a story's central conflict. This is because in reality, the central conflict has not yet been defined. Without such specific definition it is easy to become embroiled in the lead character's battles with the principle adversary. Such battles are crucial to the twists and turns of the story but they are not necessarily, in themselves, directly related to the central conflict.

As a result, the writer can find themselves mid-point in their story and realise that they don't know where the story is going. Suddenly you have lost the plot and with it the purpose of your story. A central conflict cannot be resolved if you have not managed to keep a firm grip upon it. You look at your half-finished story and all you can find is a series of battles. It is then that you find yourself asking if that was really all there ever was to your story?

Before embarking on the production of a long and involved story, it is helpful to have a good idea of the central conflict that you wish to explore. As the story takes form, a failure to identify this conflict can prove both frustrating and time consuming. At worst, it can undermine the writer to the point where the entire story is totally abandoned.

It is, therefore, useful for anyone aspiring to write a larger piece of work to develop strategies for specifying the central conflict of their story. It does not need to be very complicated, nor wordy, but it does need to be specific. Neither does it need to be clever, philosophical nor deep. The challenge can be to the lead character's physical prowess, moral qualities or a mixture of the two. Whatever the challenge, it does need to be known.

A useful strategy can be to verbalise the central conflict and then write it down. Writing it down is key as it addresses the tendency that many of us have to believe we already know the central conflict. We think we have some 'just beyond words' definition floating around in our minds. It's a little bit hazy but the writer feels its presence.

Admittedly, the words that will pin down the central conflict can be difficult to capture but that only goes to show that the strategy is worthwhile. It helps the writer to distinguish between the issues driving the sub-plots and the central issue which drives the main plot. In this way, the writer can avoid becoming deviated into a sub-plot in such a way that the real plot is lost and with it, the writer and thereby the story.

Many stories have very simple plots. This is not necessarily a bad thing. If the plot is simple then the writer is far less likely to lose sight of the central conflict. In fact, when specifying the central conflict you are probably just as well specifying your plot and sub-plot(s). You might even find it useful to tentatively define your twists (or bombs) and your resolutions. These will be covered in detail later.

To illustrate the process of specifying the central conflict in this way we can look at a simple example involving specifying a plot for a story about vampires. I will outline a plot, along with related notes, to illustrate the process. If you have difficulty with the subject for this outline, because you do not like the horror genre, then try to remember, the arch adversary could easily be a thief, murderer, philanderer, bully, rapist, confidence trickster, and so on. The only difference is, the hero might not drive a wooden stake into the heart of a confidence trickster, but then, who knows?

This outline plot revolves around an elderly man who discovers there is a vampire preying on the local villagers.

The central conflict is the good old man against the evil vampire. Tension is created by the sub-plot (we only have one in this example) which is the broken relationship with the elderly man's skeptical son. The son thinks his father is deluded and senile because his father 'stupidly' believes in myths. In such a simple story the resolutions of both sub-plot and plot (in that order) are both simple and obvious. Resolution of the sub-plot occurs when that father saves his son from the vampire and the son now realises that he was wrong about everything. The son had been a fool not to trust his father. The main plot is resolved when the father and son then unite for the final battle, with a little twist where the son ends up having to be the one who drives the stake into the vampire's heart because his father is conflicted. In the end, after bravely defeating the vampire, the father is unable to drive a wooden stake into the vampire's flesh and, without the son there to do the dirty deed, then the day would have been lost after all.

Note: You can easily add further twists (which can be delivered as bombs). This can dramatically increase tension and conflict. For example: Let the heroes discover, right at the critical moment, that the vampire is actually the living dead corpse of the old man's father. This makes our heroic duo (son and grandson of the vampire) and therefore thoroughly conflicted.

What you can see in this example is that we have clearly specified all the essential parts of our story. We know where the story is going and there is far less chance that we will become confused between tension and conflict, sub-plot and plot. We can create the tension around the sub-plot and real conflict around the main plot. We can guide the story through a maze of skirmishes and battles without ever losing sight of which one is which.

Such a strategy has also produced an extremely useful additional benefit. Since we have now distinguished sub-plot from plot, and tension from conflict, we now have a tool for starting our book. Through the use of sub-plot and tension we have determined the most important part of the back-story, namely the relationship between father and son. This back-story does nothing to explain how the old man came to know about the vampire. That is the part that we do not need to tell the reader about up-front and that is the part that many writers' guidelines seek to remove.

Many such guidelines then suggest that the best strategy to correct tedious story openings is to dive straight into the central conflict. Indeed, that may be the case for certain genres and writing styles. However, it is at least worth considering, for all the aforementioned reasons, the strategy of developing empathy with the characters through the introduction of the sub-plot. This allows the writer to plunge the reader immediately into tension, both gripping the reader and providing a small insight into the most important aspects of the back story.

Flash fiction provides a world where there is no space to fully develop a back-story prior to plunging the reader into the heart of the action. For this reason, flash fiction is an excellent tool to develop and practise the skill of writing openings. Rather than striving for eloquence, it is far better to engage your reader directly. This is often best achieved by gripping your readers with tension. As you write more, it is likely that your writing will naturally become more sophisticated. However, for those with less experience, using opening tension to carry some of your lead character's back-story, can allow readers to develop empathy with your most important characters.

3.3 Character

On my quest to improve my own writing skills I have repeatedly encountered the concept of character. In fact, there are entire books singularly devoted to this aspect of writing. Often, the treatment of character in such books spends most, or all, of the time focusing upon character description in fiction. There is a tendency to list characteristics and describe them and say how someone might act if that were them. Such books can be a useful resource if you are struggling with your characters and they will almost certainly include characteristics that you would never have thought of on your own.

However, in this book I am not going to make any attempt to duplicate or even summarise such books. You will not find any lists of characteristics here. To do so, would not be productive since anyone looking to read more about character descriptors can simply access one of the books designed specifically to meet that need.

It is easy to naively think of characters as only inhabiting fictional works. However, it is important to consider the fact that real life people are even less accessible than fictional ones. You cannot simply describe a person as they really are. That would mean knowing who someone was at some fundamental level. We do not really know others to that degree. In fact, to a degree, neither do we really know ourselves. You can know your fictional characters far better than you will ever know a real life person.

As a result, a comprehensive consideration of the characters inhabiting the pages of biographies, autobiographies and memoirs is every bit as important as the development of characters in fictional works. In reality, it can easily be argued that, dealing with the subject of character in factual based writing is far more challenging than when you have complete freedom to invent whatever characteristics your protagonists require.

In addition to a consideration of purely fictional characters, it is also useful to consider issues surrounding the use of characters which are drawn from real life. These real life characters can either be placed in their own historic setting, where real life events are detailed, or in a fictional setting, where the real life character faces fictional events. Essentially, what these two scenarios have in common is that the writer has chosen to use their intimate knowledge of a real life person to place them within a story.

There are many serious challenges to the writer whose story contains real life people engaged in real life events. In such cases, identification of the various real life people is both simple and obvious. Neither can we disregard problems arising from such obvious identification even when the people characterised in your story have already died. Everyone is part of someone's family and so the writer must pay special consideration to their own behaviour and intentions when telling such stories.

The challenge that immediately springs to mind for most people is the problem of libel, yet this is actually one of the problems that is least likely to occur. Writers who do use real people in their stories are usually so aware of libel that they are very careful to assure themselves of their own security. Permissions are sought and events or opinions are substantiated and documented where possible. Obviously, writers who choose to self-publish are unlikely to have the formal protections provided by highly experienced editors. For such writers, the only protection they really have is the care they take of the people about whom they write.

Here lies another major problem. When your characters are real people there is every chance that the characters will be recognised and someone will be upset. Once recognized, characterisations are open to dispute, and that includes the portrayal of self. It is all too easy to upset friends and family with portrayals they do not agree with, make ourselves less well considered due to a one-dimensional self-portrayal, and create real difficulties in our real world relationships.

In the end, writers themselves are also likely to be in the list of those hurt. Hurting feelings and destroying relationships is not a trivial matter. It is highly unlikely that anyone, let alone everyone, will agree with your portrayal of either themselves, or others. They may not even admit their feelings but almost everyone will feel that something is incorrect and even insulting. You can so easily damage or destroy your relationships with all sorts of other people including friends, family, the people who inhabit your story and people who know them. You may even damage third party relationships. It is a tremendous responsibility when you realise that any story based upon actual events can destroy the relationships of unforeseen countless people.

One way of countering this problem is through the manipulation of your characters so that real people are less likely to be hurt or offended. Unfortunately, this is only a partial solution as it creates a significant danger that your characterisations will appear unrealistic and shallow. The problem is really pronounced when the main conflict arises from people behaving badly rather than some non-human driven event such as a disaster. In a true story of a human caused catastrophe, no-one wants to be the one who was to blame.

At the same time, even a hero in a true story is human. Failure to include a character's limitations will almost certainly produce a lack of empathy with that character's strife. People simply do not like characters, or real people for that matter, for whom everything in life is simple and achievable because they are so brilliant. Even Superman has personal limitations. When characters do not have any limitations or failings they become remote and unrealistic. This in turn makes it much more difficult for a reader to care about a character.

When a crisis or threat is external to the central character, or characters, then it is possible to show everyone coming together to fight that external threat. In such a world, everyone

40

can be something of a hero. An example of such a story could be:

> A family sailing around the world in a small boat which sinks. The story is their struggle for life in the middle of a storm swept ocean, cramped into a tiny damaged life raft with no food or water barring that which they can glean from the uncompromising environment.

Where the threat is non-human a villain character is not essential. In true stories, such as a memoir, the threat can often arise from a sudden and dramatic change in circumstances rather than from an individual. These stories often tell of how a person, or group of people, struggle against all odds to battle the impossible. The depth of the characters arises from their very human limitations to overcome seemingly impossible obstacles. Our empathy builds because we can recognise that we too would lack the skills, endurance, bravery, stamina and determination to deal with such apparently hopeless situations. We doubt our own ability to deal with our fears, and we respect the characters for their determination to continue, despite those very same limitations.

Depth of characterisation can be particularly challenging when you personally inhabit your own story. Your own self-portrayal is critically flawed by your inherent self-bias. Regardless of the extent to which you try to counter the problem, it nevertheless remains an inescapable fact. Absolute self-honesty and self-knowledge is absolutely both illusion and delusion. No matter how deep the writer digs into their own psych, they can never be certain to surmount this problem.

In such circumstances it is extremely difficult for a writer to avoid making their own limitations feel contrived. They will need to dig deeply to admit the full extent of their least enviable attributes. They will need to fully accept that they can be cowardly, treacherous, jealous, pious, and so on. It is the way the character, who in this case is also the writer, fights against those limitations and denies them dominion, which is important. This allows readers to empathise with a character's plight. It naturally follows that, in order to struggle with your personal limitations, the writer will first need to be willing to admit such limitations to themselves. Further, they will then need to be willing to communicate their deepest hidden and least admirable characteristics to their family, friends, colleagues, neighbours and the world. This is far from a simple undertaking.

It is important to remember that, whenever a story is told about a real event, it is still telling a story. It is not the simple recounting of facts. Events, feelings, characters and situations are all seen from the writer's own personal perspective and that viewpoint is subjectively related to their beliefs, attitudes, emotions and previous experiences. No matter how hard a writer tries, it is impossible for them to simply 'tell it as it is'. As soon as anyone communicates any event to a third party it essentially becomes a fiction. A writer of that fiction needs to decide how to tackle the myriad problems that they will undoubtedly encounter.

Here is a brief summary of the key problems in non-fiction character writing:

1. We do not really know others and neither do we really know ourselves;

2. There is a danger of the writer damaging or destroying personal relationships;

3. Shallow characterization;

4. The treatment of self when the writer inhabits their own story;

5. All true stories are essentially fictions based upon real events.

In fully fictional work, most of the ideas that we have already discussed have equal significance. We need to draw our characters from somewhere and that place is our own beliefs, experiences and interpretation of the world and the people around us. We may well have real-life experience of the character traits with which we wish to imbue our story characters, but not necessarily so. We may equally have encountered character traits in other fictions. Neither is there any reason why we should not develop character traits from our imaginations based upon what we believe could possibly exist in others. We can even adopt a research-based approach where character traits are searched for in the recorded findings of psychologists, psychiatrists, counselors, anthropologists, criminologists, and so on.

Importantly, it is best not to limit the range of potential characters, and character traits, by limiting a consideration of character traits to the small world of people personally encountered by the writer. Even in an entirely fictional world, people may 'spot' themselves and be angry or upset. Not everyone will be flattered by a writer's rendition of them. Additionally, the writer's view of those other people is entirely subjective. No-one has objective access to who people really are, and a writer should never be surprised if someone doesn't agree with their personal opinion of someone they have plucked from the real world, and dropped into their fictional world.

It also strikes me as strange that, if you are going to engage your imagination to write a story, then why would you choose not to fully engage your imagination for your characters. Surely, you want your characters to be every bit as fascinating as the novel situations you create for them.

This does not mean that imagination should be unfettered. Characters should normally behave in ways that are consistent with their beliefs, morals, culture and values. Their behaviour should not be random just for the sake of surprising the reader. However, characters can still behave in ways that are unexpected, but such unexpected behaviour should still be plausible. It could appear, at first, that the behaviour was unpredictable but then the reader must feel that, actually, such behaviour was not unlikely, given the extreme and demanding circumstances within which the character found themselves.

Dialogue is a special form of action taken by your characters which allows the characters in a story to be amazingly subtle or extremely explicit about their ideas, thoughts, plans and emotions. However, amongst all the large actions, dialogue included, there are also many more very small actions that a character can make which are every bit as significant. In the story space, no action is without meaning.

Every action should say something about the characters and help readers to understand both who they are and why they behave as they do. It is only through this understanding that readers can empathise with the plight of a character. Regardless of whether they are hero, adversary or villain, they still need to be understood.

For example, in real life, you may pick up a coffee jar to make coffee and then change your mind and put it down again. Such an action may have no other significance to your life other than you decided you didn't want a coffee after all. In a story space, however, such an action must always have meaning for the character and the reader must eventually understand that meaning. The act of picking up and placing back down the coffee jar was significant to the character because it had a reason. Perhaps they are reminded of meaningful past events; or did it illustrate indecision; perhaps show a struggle with addiction, indicate a medical condition; even highlight a current tension; and so on. Every small action allows the exploration and definition of character.

The stories that are most likely to make me cry, to move me to the deepest emotion and feel the greatest empathy with the characters, are stories where there are no adversarial characters. These are stories where everyone is trying to cope with difficult circumstances but the situation is itself overwhelming. It is during the struggle against circumstances that all the character's qualities are revealed. However, many stories have adversarial characters as the principle threat. It is these adversaries that create the impossible situations through which the 'good' people must endure and eventually prevail. Such adversaries should be afforded as much attention as the heroes.

Readers need to be able to empathise with adversaries even if they do not agree with them. The characterisation must have depth and their motives must be consistent with the adversaries own problems. They do not do the terrible things they do without reason. They too have needs and desires and the reading experience vastly improves when we fully appreciate their disparate needs.

Another main character type is the villain. Even when the real adversary is the situation, a writer will often 'spice things up' with the addition of a villain in their midst. Such a character compounds any difficulties created by a situation thus making success or survival more unlikely. Such a character is truly a villain rather than an adversary. They are generally ineffectual but their actions always have the potential to create dire consequences. They will often try to sacrifice someone, or everyone, in order to save themselves or sometimes just better their own situation. When such characters exist, the writer needs also to cherish them. Sadly, treatment of the villain character is often quite shoddy and this again leads to shallow characterisation. Even villains should be interesting.

The final type of main character to mention is the victim. It is important to realise that not all stories have victims. Just because your characters are victims of aggression or challenging circumstances it does not make them victim characters. In fact, an heroic character can be victimised throughout the entire length of the story but the very nature of a hero means that they will prevail in some important sense by the end. A true victim is someone who has no way of fighting back with any efficacy and whose sole purpose is to be slaughtered or saved. How should we treat such characters?

If there are only one or two real victims in a story then the writer has a fighting chance to give the victims real lives with aspirations, purpose, personality and kinships. Readers can develop empathy with the victims and therefore experience an emotional impact when they suffer. Since it is our aim to take our readers on an intense emotional journey, then it follows that we also need to care deeply about the victims in our stories.

However, when there are larger numbers of victims, such as in disaster stories, a slightly different approach needs to be adopted. It is true that not all the victims of a disaster need to have characters. Some can simply be crushed and destroyed with as much character as the rocks which fall on their heads. But the writer will want to help the reader to generalise that such characterless victims were real people with real feelings. This is achieved through the characterisation of a number of key victims taking an active role in the story. In other words, some victim characters will have speaking parts, whilst others have simple walk on roles.

In situations where the writer attempts to characterise too many victims it becomes impossible to adequately personalise all those who play an active role in the story. Attempting such a feat often results in arbitrary characterisations for which the reader cannot develop any empathy whatsoever. In fact, a myriad of shallow victim profiles can quickly lose the reader completely. It is most definitely a case of where more is less. As a result, it is useful for those aspiring to write about large scale disasters, where there are a great number of victims, to ensure that they focus on the detailed plights of only a very few victims and thereby make each one consequential.

Building characters, regardless of whether the story is fact-based or fictional, is a tremendously exacting part of any story writing. We need to understand this fact but not allow that understanding to become overwhelming. Rather than trying to build a character all at once, it is perfectly reasonable to focus on a single aspect of a particular character and explore that using flash fiction. With repeated flashes, featuring the same character in different situations, the writer is able to build a detailed picture of the scope of behaviours that the character will produce in any new situation. Flash fiction is certainly a less daunting format than a full-length book, and therefore, a more effective way for aspiring writers to explore and develop their characters.

3.4 Point of view

One of the main concerns when writing any story is deciding the perspective from which the story will be written. This is the point of view. Every writer needs to consider the various points of view from which the story is delivered, regardless of whether their story is fictional or based upon real life events. The problem lies in the fact that you almost certainly have more than one character in your story and each of these has a point of view. In fact, beyond the story's characters there is also another point of view and that is yours, the writer. You are in the position of all seeing and all knowing. You are like a god to the finite scope of your story.

If you research 'point of view' with regards to fiction writing in other sources you may find prescriptive rules regarding what to do, and what not to do. Such rules may well be effective but I cannot dismiss the idea that some writers have the ability to break such rules. It may be the case that they can do so with such devastating brilliance that the rules are destroyed.

I much prefer the idea of making informed choices and this is very much the case with choosing your points of view. Since some people reading this book will not have considered point of view before, my aim is to outline the common choices and discuss the potential implications of those choices.

I want to start with the simplest possible story space with regards to point of view to highlight that, even in the simplest situations, point of view choices are available. Perhaps the most basic case arises from a person telling their own reminiscences of their time as an amnesia suffering hermit. Our hermit, he happens to be a man in this case, has no memory that other people exist. The hermit never sees a living soul and believes he is a unique sentient within the environment. Would it still be possible to have multiple points of view?

I think our autobiography writing hermit would still need to consider point of view when writing his story. For instance, the hermit could put himself in the mind of a lizard and tell the lizards view of events. Presumably, in such a case the lizard would become sentient, or is a lizard already sentient? He could put himself in the mind of a rock and tell the rock's view of events and then even the rock might be considered sentient too. He can even put himself in the position of an 'all seeing all knowing entity' and tell the story from the position of simultaneously knowing everything from the point of view of all things. Even in this limited world, point of view is a choice. The point of view can switch or stay the same throughout. The important point is that the writer should always be consciously aware of the current point of view and only change that point of view as a deliberate decision.

If you are just starting on your writing career then you may not have considered the idea of choosing a point of view. You may even have considered point of view as obvious or self-determining; almost as if the point of view chooses itself. I hope you can now see that it does not. It is for the writer to choose the stance from which a story is told and it is useful to make those choices informed ones.

The hermit example highlights the fact that point of view is just as much an issue for those wishing to write a factual story based upon their own life as it is for those aiming to write pure fiction. Many of the people who would like to write a book believe that their real lives are interesting and would like to tell their own story. The problem lies in the fact that many of these aspiring writers are totally untrained. As a result, some such writers will believe that point of view is not a consideration for them since it is obvious; they want to write their story from their own personal viewpoint. If you fall into this category then I hope that the hermit example has helped you to be aware that point of view is a choice, regardless of your story. Knowing this fact allows aspiring writers to think more creatively about how they might go about telling their stories.

The most powerful viewpoint with regards to what can be told is the omniscient view. This is the point of view that we touched upon earlier where the writer tells a story from the position of an all seeing, all knowing entity. It allows the writer to deliver the entire story no matter which characters are present to witness events. You are in a position to tell the reader what everyone is thinking and doing at all times. The lead character does not need to be there or even have any awareness that the described events have taken place.

In fact, technically there is no need to have any witnesses to events. Perhaps the only character present is sleeping and remains asleep throughout the event, or even lying unconscious in a hospital bed. The writer can even report and describe events that happened where no living thing at all is present. The omniscient view provides a god's eye view of everything that is going on as it actually happens. We can intimately know everything that is in the hearts and minds of every single character in the story.

As a result, the omniscient writer can even report the feelings or thoughts of several characters at the same time, for example: 'Peter was frightened but Sally knew he was over-reacting'. Here we have simultaneous access to unobservable events occurring for two different characters. The feelings and thoughts are stated rather than interpreted from some outwardly observable actions or behaviour. Even more omnisciently, the writer can say what whole groups of characters are thinking and feeling, for example 'Everyone was frightened even though they all knew it was an over-reaction'.

As you can see, the omniscient point of view is powerful and, therefore, a useful tool to have at your disposal. Sadly, as you may have guessed, there are significant drawbacks to the overuse of this approach which relate to the reader's involvement with the characters. In order to develop a deep empathy with your characters, the reader needs to be as close to the character's world as possible. This is particularly true for the central character. The problem with the omniscient point of view is that it does not facilitate such closeness.

The other options for point of view, in decreasing levels of closeness, are: first person (I); second person (you); and third person (he, she, it). First person is most intimate, because we are seeing the world directly through the eyes of a specific character, and third person is least intimate, because we are reading a report of what happened to someone else.

Some books offering guidelines to those wishing to improve their writing skills ignore second person point of view. This is probably because their focus is purely on fiction where the use of second person is uncommon and can be challenging to use. However, I am not going to discount second person point of view because it is used frequently in fact-based writing. When you write in the second person, it makes your writing apply directly to your reader. This book is, loosely speaking, a fact-based book and often makes use of a second person viewpoint. In fact, I am using a combination of first person and second person points of view whilst addressing you throughout this paragraph.

Second person point of view can also help to create a sense of personal urgency when writing a story. The reader is pulled into the story so that they can start to feel part of the action, almost as if it was the reader's own story that was being told. For example:

You're desperate. You see the old man is done. Bloodless skin, thin over bone and delving into deep pits of his eyes and cheeks. His closed eyelids flicker briefly. He's alive. You move to shake him awake. Your hand stops a whisker away from the old man's shoulder. You can't do it. Paralysed by a sudden feeling. What is stopping you?

I see no reason why you should not feel free to experiment with writing in the second person. Flash provides an ideal story format for such experimentation and it allows you to find out if second person is a viewpoint that helps you to meet your writing objectives.

There is also the cinematic point of view where the writer describes scenes as if filmed by a camera. Using this point of view, we are able to describe everything in the scene, irrespective of whether characters can see the described details. This differs from the omniscient view in that the camera can only see objects, actions and events. It cannot see thoughts and emotions and so they need to be surmised by the reader from the described actions and events.

When a writer wishes to maximise closeness, and thereby empathy, he or she will usually adopt the first person point of view. It is almost always adopted for fact-based stories such as memoirs and auto-biographies but it is also commonly used for fictional works. First person point of view allows the characters themselves to tell the reader what is happening. From this perspective, everything that the point of view character sees, touches, hears, smells, tastes, feels and thinks, is all described by the point of view character themselves. It is not possible to be closer to the character's experience and, when executed well, the reader starts to think and feel along with the point of view character.

To illustrate this idea the following example is kept deliberately simple:

My ears strain into the darkness but I can't hear a sound, just the blood pounding in my ears.

Notice that, even without the context, you feel close to the significant emotional impact that the quietness is having on our character. In other words, we have already started to build an empathetic relationship. It would not be possible for anyone else to hear the characters blood and so we are given an intimate insight delivered through a character's personal experience.

Empathy is further enhanced when the reader is only required to empathise with a single character throughout an entire story. In such stories we stay within the lead character throughout the story, feeling and experiencing along with them. There is no confusion regarding with whom we are empathising most deeply, and this approach facilitates the production of intense emotional reactions in our readers.

Third person point of view is where the writer tells the story through one of the characters. Although events and experiences are seen from the viewpoint of a character, it is the writer who is telling the story. It is a very common strategy that is used by many successful writers of fiction.

To illustrate the difference between first person and third person I have used the same example as used for first person, but in this case, told from third person point of view:

His ears strain into the darkness but he can't hear a sound, just the blood pounding in his ears.

Here, the writer's voice is coming between the character and the experiences of that character. We still feel close to the significant emotional impact that the quietness is having on our character, however, we are just that little bit further removed. We still have access to the sound of blood, but now the writer is telling us that the character is hearing it, rather than the character telling us himself. In other words, in third person point of view, we can say what the point of view character thinks and feels and also say what they are able to see or witness but it is not the character themselves who is telling the story. It is not quite as intimate as telling the story in the first person.

It is not just the point of view that is open to change but also the point of view character. One part of a story can be told through one character whilst the next part of the story can be told through the eyes of another. Theoretically, there is no limit to the number of characters that are made point of view characters within the telling of a single story.

A problem that can arise when adopting several characters as point of view characters, particularly for those with less writing experience, is that it is quite easy to lose track of who is actually the main character. Switching between various point of view characters in an unplanned and disorganised way is a practise sometimes referred to as head-hopping. One moment you are in the head of one character and a moment later you're in a different character. If the writer is totally disorganised then it is likely that the reader will also lose track of both characters and story. It becomes impossible for a reader to identify the central character.

Here is a simple example where the point of view character is switched within a sentence along with associated comments provided in brackets:

Jon looked up from the pitch and ran his eyes around the crowded football stadium. (The point of view character is established as Jon, allowing us to know what is happening inside him.) He was thrilled by the adrenaline saturated atmosphere but Jenny's adrenaline was having a very different effect. (The point of view has been switched mid-sentence so that we are now able to see the story world through the character Jenny.) She just wanted to run from the revolting, sweating mass of humanity which crushed all around her. (We have full access to the world from Jenny's perspective.)

It is not just the danger of both writers and readers becoming confused which creates the problems. We also need to consider the effect switching point of view has on the reader's relationships with characters. We want to build feelings of empathy within the reader but we cannot expect them to simultaneously empathise with everyone. The more different character viewpoints that are adopted, the weaker the emotional bond that is created between reader and characters. This is unlikely to produce the best results because the main objective is to invoke real emotions within our readers.

However, occasions do arise where the writer of a story will feel it appropriate to switch to a different point of view character. For example, a writer may have worked hard to help readers develop strong emotional bonds with the lead character through the use of the first person point of view. The plot then requires something to happen which the lead character does not witness. If it is reasonable for the lead to find out about the event then the writer can simply have some other character tell them about it. The lead character could also find out through a newspaper, or surmise events must have taken place from other evidence which is available to the lead character.

In circumstances where the writer wants the reader to know about an event, yet still conceal that event from a first person lead, then the point of view character will need to change. However, the change in point of view character is a deliberate choice on the part of the writer and not simply something that has happened due to insufficient attention to detail. In this situation, a writer can choose to write an entire scene from any other viewpoint they desire. It could be that another character is used to deliver their first person view of events but equally, an omniscient view, or even a second or third person viewpoint, could be adopted. Provided the writer consciously decides when a change in point of view is to occur, and also strictly limits the number and frequency of such changes, then there is no reason why multiple points of view cannot be used.

When starting a longer piece of work, one of the useful decisions that can be made, ahead of starting to write, is the overall point of view that will be adopted. This will not preclude the use of other points of view but it will make it less likely that the writer will find themselves half way through writing a book and suddenly decide that it all needs to be re-written from another viewpoint. The flash short story model can help greatly in making this decision. Major scenes from a larger work can be written as flash fictions. This allows the experimental assessment of a variety of viewpoints so that an informed decision can be made as to which viewpoint is preferred for the writing task at hand.

3.5 Dialogue

The subject of dialogue, as 'talking' is referred to when discussed in the context of writing, can often be difficult for aspiring writers. Although I always played with dialogue, my original working life as a research-based factual writer afforded little opportunity to use dialogue in my professional work. As a result, when I started to use dialogue more frequently, I began by researching examples of dialogue from a wide range of books. I was careful to include books that I did not enjoy in order to identify patterns and writing styles that could inform my own writing.

It did not take long for me to realise that there is tremendous variety in the forms, styles and uses of written speech. It was apparent that when writers of technical books on writing are discussing dialogue, they are in fact referring to conversation and written speech in all its colourful forms. In addition to simple conversations between two people, it is useful to explicitly explore group conversations as well as conversations where only a single character speaks.

When learning to write conversations it is probably a good idea to start with conversations involving just two people. This allows an aspiring writer to concentrate on using spoken words for: character development; tension and conflict creation; building context; exploding bombs; and reaching resolution. Each of these is discussed in more detail under various other guidelines presented in this chapter. Nevertheless, it is important to understand that the action of speaking is likely to play an essential part in developing the reader's empathetic link with all the other crucial elements of any story.

All speech is an interaction. Even if a character is speaking in their head (a conscious form of verbalised thinking), they are interacting, even if it is with themselves. More importantly, speech creates interactions between characters and readers. If, for example, you want to tell your reader what your character is thinking then you, as the writer, can choose to tell them. Alternatively, you can let the character themselves tell the reader what they are thinking by verbalising their thoughts. This produces a written monologue but as far as your reader's experience goes, they feel that they are in dialogue with your character. In fact, they are. Your characters are communicating directly with the reader.

You can experiment with monologue in all sorts of ways to place the reader in the room with your character's inner most thoughts, ideas, feelings and emotions. You can have your characters talk into their coffee mug, shout at the storm, or confess to a gravestone. All these forms of speech give direct access to your character in a way which can capture the reader and build their empathy with your key protagonists.

It is not only inanimate objects that can be used as the recipient of your character's utterances. Animals, and particularly pets, are often considered sentient and so, although the animal does not talk back directly, they can communicate non-verbally using gestures and expressions. It may even be appropriate, within the context of your story, to have your character verbalise for an animal. Since this may be difficult to visualise immediately, here is an example of a man talking with his dog.

"You wouldn't tell me to leave would you Fred. No, not you. If I petted another dog you'd forgive me right off. You'd just wag your tail and say, 'Give me a pat too.'"

People living on their own often talk to their pets and regard them in much the same way that they would regard another human being. In fact, the relationship can often be even more intimate. Animals can provide useful confidants, co-conspirators, adversaries, friends, or any number of other roles, effectively making them characters in their own right.

A relatively novel use of monologue is employed in the film, Sixth Sense. Throughout the film, the lead character talks to numerous people who appear to be engaged in conversation with him. It is only at the end that you realise that the other people never actually spoke back. In fact, the lead character is a ghost and most people are unable to see, feel or hear him. Nevertheless, the words that he speaks can be heard by the viewer, or reader, and through the words that he utters, the audience builds their relationship with him.

Dealing with multiple people talking at once can be a headache for both the writer and the subsequent reader. The number of people actively engaging in a conversation at any one time, therefore, should be small. Other characters may be in the conversation but, just as in life, it's probably best not to have them all speak at once. It does happen on occasion in life but it is not the ideal way of communicating. In a group, conversation often flows for stable periods through just two or three active speakers with the occasional small interjections from others. Any serious interjection is likely to lead to a change in the key two or three actively involved speakers.

In flash fiction, where you have an extremely limited number of words to convey your story, too many characters actively involved in a conversation is likely to lead to total confusion for both writer and reader. Often the active involvement of three characters can be essential to carry your story but there would rarely be a situation where more than three active participants in a conversation would be essential, or even desirable.

Through the process of critically thinking about the mechanisms used in the works of other fiction writers, we can identify some of the key styles of written speech that we personally enjoy and other styles which, if we are honest with ourselves, we either do not like or we are unable to even read. In fact, I enjoy narrative writing and often find myself moved from the greatest wonder to the deepest sadness, and even tears, when reading the narrative descriptions of a person's experience of real life events. Such narratives need not include any dialogue at all.

What constitutes good dialogue and good written speech for your own personal taste, does not necessarily apply as a general rule for everyone. For example, I do not particularly enjoy dialect and therefore I keep the use of dialect in my writing to an absolute minimum. In fact, I would only ever use dialect when it was absolutely essential to the understanding of a particular event or interaction. Even then, I would only use a few key words of dialect to provide a flavour rather than trying to mimic the actual dialect.

At the same time, I am fully aware that this is not true of all readers and writers. For instance, the award winning and highly regarded writer, Roddy Doyle, uses dialect extensively in his work. Roddy Doyle's work has great merit even if it does not suit all readers. As a result, in my writing the use of dialect in written conversation is kept to a minimum but for other writers it must be down to their own personal decision.

Effective results can be achieved with dialect when it is used sparingly. This allows you to deliver the essence of characters and situations without risking losing your way, or your readers, especially if you are a writer who finds using dialect challenging.

One of the most common pieces of advice proffered, with regard to dialogue, is that the speech of characters should be naturalistic. Conversations should sound real. This does not mean that the content of conversations should be real, content can be anything. It means that the words spoken by each character should be consistent with that character. It also means that the structure, the ebbs and flows of the conversation, should also feel natural.

However, this does not mean predictable. In fact, good dialogue is unpredictable. As a writer, you are contriving your character's speech in order to render your story or plot, even when that story or plot is based on real events. If your character's words feel contrived then you risk irritating the reader and this can cause them to stop reading your story.

Naturalistic conversation includes a wide range of twists and turns that seem to follow one another. When conversations are analysed, however, those twists and turns often do not directly follow at all. People often talk at cross purposes. They make links with previously un-introduced topics. Sometimes a person will try to change the subject or they will make tangential link that may have the effect of changing the subject. In fact, there are all manner of ways that a writer can surprise their readers by using the naturalistic twists and turns that are common in real conversations.

At the same time, it is likely to confuse the reader if you use unpredictability just for the purpose of being unpredictable. Such an approach will lead to random conversation which does not serve any purpose within your story. You should be trying to achieve something so that, even when your characters are talking at cross purposes, each is talking within the context of their own needs, feelings and agendas. Conversation is never random either in writing or in real life.

Once you have decided how you will use dialogue in your current writing task you will still need to carefully consider how you let your reader know who is speaking. This is further complicated by the fact that the various characters can be in different emotional states and can therefore be speaking in very different tones. What happens, for example, if one character is deliberately annoying another who is responding with anger? The tones used by the two characters to deliver their words will be very different and this must be communicated to the reader.

In the past a wide range of speech tags were used to achieve this and indeed, the use of a great variety of tags was deemed acceptable.

Examples of speech tags include:

he said; she shouted; he whispered; she intoned; he confided; I replied; she confessed; she chastised; he chided; he droned; she colluded; I joked; she intimated; she suggested; he explained; he demanded; he pleaded; she ruminated; I persuaded; he implied; and so on.

Many modern writers now feel that the use of multiple speech tags should be limited or even excluded altogether. It is often felt that multiple tags are distracting or may even be counter-productive to the readers interpretation of poorly crafted situations, thus creating a disconnect between readers and characters. If the scene is correctly crafted then the reader already knows who is speaking and the tone that they are using. If the reader knows that a character needs to shout, and the words are consistent with that action, then you do not need to add the 'he/she shouted' speech tag. Even more problematic, if your reader has not understood that a character needs to shout, because the setting has not been crafted with sufficient care, then the reader will have their understanding derailed by the use of a speech tag presented after the speech, which is inconsistent with their expectations.

A strict approach to this problem involves only ever using the tag 'said' and even this is used sparingly just to help the reader keep track of who is actually speaking during long runs of dialogue. The purist argument is, if the image created in the reader's mind has been constructed with adequate care and attention to detail then the reader already knows both who is speaking and how exactly the words are spoken without needing to be explicitly told after the fact.

Characters rarely stand still, facing each other, speaking and making no other movement whatsoever. When sentient entities interact verbally, they are usually doing something else at the same time. Remember, a writer can choose to imbue any creature or object with sentient and animate properties. At the very least, we would expect the simultaneous display of some form of gestural non-verbal communication. Even the fixed features of a sentient being which has no emotion is, itself communicating this fact non-verbally. These are all actions and the reader needs to understand these actions in order to interpret the written utterances. At the same time, these actions can help to keep track of the sentient being that is actually speaking, as well as their emotional state. All such actions can be turned into action tags for speech. For example:

Harry looked down at the small revolver cradled in his hands. "I'm so weary."
He shook his head. How had things come to this? From the corner of his eye he noticed a movement and in a flash turned the revolver on his boss.
"Don't you come any closer."
"Look Harry, I was just trying to help."

In that short conversation we know exactly who is speaking and the emotions behind the words even though speech tags are not used. Even in a simple example such as this, where we have not been introduced to a back story, the characters, their emotions, or the situation, the reader is still able to know who is speaking, their tone and the relationship between the characters. There are no speech tags to distance the reader from the action and so the reader is drawn directly into the intensity of the situation, allowing them to imagine witnessing the interaction between the characters involved.

Additionally, many modern writers, and critics, find the use of adverbs to modify the speaking verb, even less tolerable. A simple example might be, he shouted angrily. A more complicated example is, she refuted adamantly. As previously mentioned, the reader should already know how the words are spoken before reading them. Modifying the verb only serves to remove the reader from the immediacy of the scenes emotion.

In the final assessment you, as the writer, will need to choose how you tag your dialogue to let the reader know who is speaking. When making that choice, it is important to be under no illusion that such apparently minor decisions do have major impacts on the reader and how they experience your writing in the moment.

The complexity of the way writers use dialogue to deliver their stories has necessitated this long section even though I have kept the detail and examples to an absolute minimum. Nevertheless, this has been an important topic because dialogue often plays a central role in delivering stories to readers. In the word limited world of flash fiction, a few spoken words can sometimes deliver more tension, mood, emotion and story than would be affected through narrative alone and so flash writing provides a useful tool for practising your dialogue writing style.

3.6 Show or tell?

When telling a story, one of the key choices a writer needs to make is the balance between showing and telling. In many cases, 'show don't tell' is a mantra presented as an absolute rule of good writing style which can apply to both fictional and non-fictional works. However, showing can be significantly enhanced when supported by the appropriate use of telling.

Telling makes extensive use of adjectives to describe what happens and what it means to the characters involved. The reader is not required to interpret what the characters are feeling from the events in which they are involved because the writer is able to state exactly what those feelings are.

Showing, on the other hand, presents the actual behaviours, both actions and reactions, of the characters and allows the reader to interpret the motives and feelings of characters from those behaviours. The characters are seen to be behaving in ways that are not simply consistent with their emotions, but are actually indicative of those emotions.

For the aspiring writer, telling can often feel like the best way of letting the reader know what is in the mind's eye of the writer. For such writers, the focus is often placed almost entirely on 'painting a picture with words'. In other words, all of the writing effort is directed at producing imaginative, eloquent and highly detailed descriptions.

The major limitations with such an approach are that long descriptions will tend to: slow story progress which can prove tedious; result in cliché rather than eloquence; and rather than bring the reader closer to the scene, can distance the reader since they are not actively involved. In other words, the writer leaves the reader nothing to interpret. Irrespective of a scene's tension and drama, the reader is still being told about it indirectly, rather than feeling it. This can easily produce both emotional distance and disinterest for the reader.

For a reader to fully engage emotionally with a scene or event they need to be guided into a state of empathy. Only in this way are they able to internalize and really feel a place or situation. This can most easily be achieved through showing the experiences of the characters and allowing the reader to actively engage in the interpretation of their actions and reactions. The reader must be helped to empathise, and thereby experience an emotional interaction with the characters and the events. To achieve this, the reader is shown events through the characters senses and emotions so that they can discover the scene in real time with the characters inhabiting the story. The reader sees, hears, smells, tastes, touches and feels through the character's immediate interactions with the story environment.

The difference between these approaches is perhaps best illustrated by a simple example:

A telling approach to a scene may look like this:

There was a single chair standing in the middle of the darkened room. George felt frightened.

A telling approach with additional descriptive detail may read like this:

There was a solitary dining style chair, with a squat wooden slatted back reminiscent of 1960's design and a plush upholstered seat base which looked to be still intact. The four turned legs, braced by cross members, were planted at an oblique angle in the middle of the entirely gloom filled room. George thought it was as though a shadow had entered this place and would never leave.

A showing approach to the same scene may look like this:

George gradually made out a shape in the darkened room. It was a chair. A shiver shook his body.

In the first two cases, we are told exactly what is in the room and how George feels about what is in the room. Despite the simplicity of description in the first case, the reader is not invited to imagine or interpret. Their view of the scene is left in a simple state.

In the second case, the additional description does provide the reader with a much more detailed image of the scene but still does not require the reader to invoke their imagination or make any interpretations. Again, the reader has access to all the pertinent details.

In the final instance, even though readers are not given time to develop real empathy with George, they are still more likely to have an emotional response to the scene. This is because the scene is delivered through George's direct experience of his surroundings. We see George's physical reaction to the scene and must imagine and interpret his emotions from the combination of George's experiences and his physical reactions to those experiences. In this way, readers become actively involved in the events that are taking place.

Of course we can drive home the interpretations made by the reader with the use of some telling. In the final case, the simple adding of a telling half sentence completes the scene:

George gradually made out a shape in the darkened room. It was a chair. A shiver shook his body as shock and fear engulfed him.

There are also occasions where you wish to describe events that would not normally be directly experienced by your character. Nevertheless, such events still play a crucial part in your story and you still want your readers to be able to empathise with the emotional and physical impact of such events on your characters. If you have worked hard at building empathy for your characters then you certainly would not want to lose them through poor narrative. Hopefully, the degree of relationship that you have built with your readers will make them much more tolerant. Nevertheless, it is not a good idea to push that tolerance too far.

In order to convert a remote event into an experience, we can allow our characters to become aware of these events through their interactions with others, or even through their interpretations of any evidence that they encounter. The beauty of this is that it is then possible to show your characters reacting to events which they did not personally experience first-hand. Your characters can experience the full gamut of emotions which you can show through the words they speak and the actions they make.

Again, however, it is all too easy to fall into the position of telling everything and showing nothing. Too much telling can instantly lose any immediacy that you have created.

For example, upon entering the room containing the chair you could tell the reader:

George was upset by the empty chair because he knew that he was too late.

Rather than showing:

George slammed a clenched fist into his own forehead. "No. Please God, no. Oh God. I'm too late."

The evidence of the empty chair allows George to know about the terrible thing that happened in that room, even if the reader still does not know. By showing George's reactions to what he has seen, you have not only allowed the reader to empathise with the emotions of your character but you have also been able to convey the tremendous importance of the event. Your character isn't just upset. In fact, their entire world has just been turned upside down.

In flash writing, there is insufficient space to develop empathy using telling alone. However, if you wish to use flash to outline an entire story for a much larger work then a significant amount of telling will be essential. This is because telling can allow the outlining of ideas without too much detailed exposition. Neither would such an outline require too much description. An awareness of your goals for an individual flash piece is essential.

Showing, on the other hand, facilitates the building of pace, intensity, emotion and empathy. The flash writing format requires that this is executed with an economical, and therefore precise, use of words. This is true regardless of whether your work is fictional or biographical. Flash facilitates experimentation with showing and telling so that we can better understand the balance between showing and telling in the way we choose to deliver our stories.

3.7 Expectations

Ensuring readers are willing to stick around to the end of the story is the main challenge for any writer, including writers of fact-based stories. We strive to keep the audience involved all the way through to the time when we are ready to deliver the reader from all their fears and doubts. Everything we have discussed to this point has been aimed at this objective. Irrespective of how much care was taken over characters and their dialogue, creating tension and conflict, or invoking empathy, the truth is that many readers will not be pulled along without suspense.

Readers must experience anticipation. Somewhere, even if it is within their subconscious minds, they need to feel unsure. Readers need uncertainty; they need an active experience; they need to be involved. If the reader is experiencing empathy then that involvement can only be heightened by the addition of suspense.

To invoke suspense, it is important that the audience is not constantly feeling, 'I knew that was coming'. It is far better for your readers to have no expectations at all, than to have every expectation constantly confirmed.

When we talk about suspense we are really talking about expectations. The reader needs to be in a state of expectation. Once in that state, they are vulnerable to all sorts of perturbations that the writer can chose to unleash upon them.

They need to expect that something will happen but whether something does happen is entirely up to the writer. In a state of expectation, the reader finds it very difficult to stop reading until they know what happens next.

A reader is unlikely to be sufficiently concerned about the characters in a story to experience suspense unless that reader has developed some empathetic feelings towards those characters. Such empathy can be developed extremely rapidly. Simply placing a character in an uncertain position can be sufficient to initiate some empathy. In a state of suspense, not knowing what will happen next, the change of state can arise from anything - from nothing happening, right through to a cataclysmic overturning of the world order that your story has already established.

Expectations can be heightened, and often are, as much by inaction as they are by action. Two small girls stand in the corridor of the Overlook Hotel in Stephen King's The Shining. They don't actually do anything but the reader can't help but expect that they might. An oriental priest, trained in martial arts, is harangued by ruffians. We expect him to defend himself but he demonstrates his fearlessness by his passivity. A massive storm heads for a group of castaways adrift in a life raft. They can do nothing but await its arrival.

These are all examples of where inaction helps to build the reader's expectation. In fact, this is classic suspense and it is often at its most intense when action is totally absent. Here is an even simpler example:

Not a thing stirred in the darkened house.

The very fact that we have stated that there is nothing moving implies that something might move at any moment, and with dire consequences.

Building the reader's expectations is every bit as important when writing fact-based stories as it is in fictional work. Once we have worked hard to build expectation we still need to do something with it. Beginning memoir writers need to pay particular notice of this point. It is not uncommon for inexperienced writers to create what amounts to little more than a list of events taking the form of: 'I did this, then I did that, then the other.' This does nothing to build reader expectations.

It does not follow that serious consequences will result from every situation. Sometimes there are totally innocent reasons why, for example, 'there is nothing stirring in the house.' It is important to strike a balance between how some expectations are explained away whilst others result in massively deteriorating situations for the story's characters. Balance keeps the reader on their toes each time they encounter raised expectations.

When real life events occur, there may not have been discernible plots or sub-plots. Events are often unrelated in the scientific sense of cause and effect. In order for the people who experience those events to make sense of them they need to construct an underlying pattern to the events. In effect, events, and people's reactions to those events, link together into a story that takes on the apparent formation of discernible plots and sub-plots. Memoir writers need to tune into this process so that their memoirs present the story rather than a list of events.

Every time a writer plays out a situation where expectations have been heightened they are in fact working with surprises. These are not the big plot surprises but they are surprises nonetheless. They can be large or small but in any case, expectations should have been built in such a way that, when something does happen, the reader must either not have expected it, or even have expected something completely different. Even so, the event must still be believable.

The placement of surprises, sometimes referred to as twists, helps to keep an audience slightly unbalanced whilst the writer develops the main plot and themes where the important surprises will occur. Sometimes, writers use the term surprise to refer to the major story twists but this almost denies the existence of the smaller events that also disrupt either the main plot or a sub-plot. Surprises allow the writer to end a section with the reader wanting answers. The event is introduced but never immediately resolved. It allows for the creation of that indispensible situation where the reader is desperate to know what happens next.

When referring to the few truly significant surprises in a story we can use the idea of bombs. The reason I want to distinguish between surprises, which merely unsettle the lead character, and bombs, which totally undermine almost every chance the lead character has to endure, is that the latter has major story implications. The idea of surprise vastly understates the impact of such events.

As a writer, you will probably want to detonate a 'bomb' under your reader once in a while. You will have carefully gathered together your bomb making materials, all the while acting as nonchalantly as possible so that nobody suspects what you are up to. You will have provided excuses to explain any unusual behaviours and you will have built your bomb with all the craft and care that you would if it were a real bomb that could easily blow up in your face during the building of it. You will then, as secretly as possible, go out and plant your bomb in the perfect place. Then, just as your reader arrives at the end of your chapter, **bang**, you detonate the bomb right under every assumption that they hold. You literally turn the story world upside down.

Bombs are devices that can be employed in a number of ways depending upon the purpose that you wish them to serve. They can be used to make resolutions seem absolutely impossible or to create situations where resolutions becomes possible. Regardless of the use of a bomb, it should have certain key characteristics.

1. If the reader were Sherlock Holmes, then it would have been possible for them to work out that the bomb existed, where it was planted and when it would be detonated. At the very least, the event should have credulity. It should feel honest.

2. Since no-one is Sherlock Holmes, then the major upheaval must come as a complete surprise. This in itself is surprising, since any good read will take the reader on an emotional roller-coaster by systematically pulling the ground from under the main character with whom they have developed so much empathy.

3. A purpose must be served by the shock. If the event seems random and has no immediate bearing on the situation, or the lead character, then it is likely that the reader will rightly question the stories authenticity. In other words, it must have immediate dramatic significance.

Bombs do not create expectations but they do ensure that readers learn to fear their expectations because it makes it possible that absolutely anything can happen at any time. Crucially, bombs either massively damage, or apparently destroy, the lead character's chances of surviving intact from their physical, social or psychological ordeals.

Even memoirs and biographies have dramatic events which wreak havoc on the life of the subject. If that was not the case, the writer in you would probably feel that the story was not of sufficient interest to record. Obviously, in real life, we have no control over dramatic events. They occur when and how the real events unfolded. However, that is not to say that the writer has no control over their exposition. On the contrary, it is the writer's job to expose dramatic events in such a way that the reader understands the enormous impact that such events have on the lead character. This can be just as true in many fact-based stories as it is in fiction.

In dramatic fiction, bombs are often placed with methodical attention to detail. One is planted near the start of the story to set up the principle plot dilemma, then another one goes off in the middle to deteriorate the lead character's position, and then a final bomb is detonated towards the end which removes any fleeting hope that the lead character might still hold. This sets up the perfect Houdini trick where the lead character overcomes their inevitable doom and instead succeeds, in one form or another. Even in death, a purpose must have been served where the lead character overcomes in some way.

An example from a real-life story, where the death of the lead characters is triumphant nonetheless, is the story telling of the trek by Robert Falcon Scott and his party of Antarctic explorers. Scott and his party of men, set out to be the first people to reach the South Pole. They failed when a group of Norwegian explorers beat them to the Pole. Then, while the defeated Scott was trying to return home, the entire party froze to death. It was failure compounded by the ultimate failure, death.

Yet the story of Scott of the Antarctic is much loved and this is due to the way that the story is told. The final bomb is detonated in the story when, critically low on supplies, the Antarctic weather closes in. The explorers endure the most unspeakable conditions with such bravery that they are even willing to sacrifice their own lives so that those remaining might have the smallest chance of survival. Against all odds, Scott and his party of explorers displayed incredible bravery, endurance and moral courage whilst making the ultimate sacrifice, that of their lives. This was the success of their human spirit and there is nothing more moving than that. Even in death, our lead characters can emerge victorious.

In the same way that flash fiction can be used to create the tense mini-stories that are played out within a major story, it can also be used to work through events which are so explosive, they are capable of changing the entire direction of the story. One of the greatest problems for you, as an aspiring writer, is working out the bigger picture. What is the story? Even when depicting real-life events the story is not obvious. The writer must find that story in order to write it. Thinking and working through the story's key turning points can both dramatically help, and help dramatically. The use of flash fiction for finding the real bombs, in other words, the true turning points in a real-life story is every bit as helpful as when used in a fictional context.

3.8 Resolutions

Every story introduces problems and challenges for the characters. When you think about real life, problems often arise which have no immediate solution. The presenting issue becomes either a challenge or a worry. In life, this is not what we would normally want. We want our problems solved quickly so that we can continue meeting new challenges without the continuing worry of situations that remain unresolved. Without resolutions, our problems build up and become stressors. If the number and intensity of stressors increases beyond the capacity for a person to cope then the result is often psychological ill-health and breakdown. This in turn leads to both behavioural and social changes which can isolate a person further and lead to long term health issues or even suicide.

On the other hand, just as we do not want a build up in the number and intensity of stressors in real life, in the story world, this is exactly what we do want. If problems are instantly resolved then they are not problems at all. When we read a story, factual or fictional, we want to see, feel, understand and empathise with the characters when they face their life challenges. This can only be achieved when challenges remain unresolved. Unresolved challenges raise expectations. Resolved challenges, on the other hand, remove the anticipation the reader feels and, as a result, it removes the opportunity for them to care. If you undermine the reader's capacity to care for the characters in your story then you remove their motivation. You want readers to feel that they need to know what happens next. It is that feeling that keeps the pages turning.

Since we need unresolved challenges, it is normal for several unresolved problems to build up throughout a long story. These challenges fall into two basic categories: challenges directly related to the main plot; and challenges related to any sub-plots in your story. There may also be an overarching theme in the story, for example: selfless love; inevitable death; tenuous faith; or corruptive power; and so on. If so, then the main challenges faced by the story's lead characters should also shed light on their relationship with that theme. In this way, the writer can ensure that the sub-plots and the main plot are congruent. Even if sub-plots are only obliquely relevant to the main plot they still allow the reader to gain insight into character as a personal quality, and specifically the character of the story's principle characters.

It may seem contradictory but readers also want and need answers. While it is true that there are many books where a number of challenges have been left unresolved, even in the final conclusion of the story, such stories tend to have an amateur feel to them. That is not to say that they cannot be enjoyable just the same. However, literary critics are not usually as forgiving as the average reader. As a result, it is usually the best policy to resolve all the struggles that you have introduced even if the resolution is, in reality, an explanation of how a struggle could not be resolved. This means that it is usually helpful if sub-plots are not left simply hanging or unresolved after the story has been completed. It tends to leave the reader at least a little dissatisfied.

There are a variety of ideas on when and where plots and sub-plots should be resolved. Sometimes these ideas look and feel extremely formulaic. Obviously the resolution of the main plot needs to come towards the end of a story but, in practise, writers have a choice of exactly how, when and where. Sometimes, sub-plots are resolved before the main plot, sometimes after, and at other times the resolution of the sub-plots and the main plot coincide. Although, as I already stated, the main plot resolution does come towards the end of a story, it is not usually the final word and some wrapping up is often required afterwards.

There are various ways of resolving remaining issues so that a story feels natural and complete. For instance, this can be achieved with a wrapping up section within the story or it can be dealt with by presenting the missing details in a postscript. Some readers do not read a preface or a postscript, where one is present, and so placing important information in such structures can mean that the reader may miss a crucial message or part of the story.

This is particularly the case if a final twist in the theme, rather than the plot, is placed in a postscript. Readers who do not read postscripts will then miss the philosophically most important part of the story. An example, with which many readers will be familiar, of a postscript used for this purpose can be found in Yann Martel's 'Life of Pi'. For those who have not read the book, I will not spoil the story by revealing Martel's final twist.

However, rather than concentrating on exactly when or where you resolve the plot and sub-plots, it is far more important to concentrate on how you resolve them. The aim is to deliver salvation. Even if the main character loses everything, including their friends, family, life and soul, they must still leave a positive legacy. They may have retained something important in the face of ultimate loss such as their dignity, bravery, artistry, loyalty, and so on. In other words, the reader is guided towards a place where they can discover a satisfying resolution. It's a place where all the conflict suddenly makes perfect sense to both the story's characters and the reader.

Here is a checklist of some of the main points to consider when resolving plots and sub-plots, and also a theme if you have one.

1. Sub-plots, plots and themes should be resolved in some way.

2. The lead character should not find it easy to resolve their problems or struggles.

3. Struggles should not be resolved by chance or luck. Stories work best when the lead actively engages with their problems and only through their extraordinary efforts is resolution reached.

4. Resolution does not require a complete answer but even the smallest sub-plot should not simply be forgotten or ignored.

5. When something is left incompletely resolved then it should be a deliberate act by the writer for the purpose of taking the reader on a cognitive journey beyond the pages of the story.

6. If you have a theme, it is an achievement if you can leave it resolved in terms of the story whilst, at the same time, leaving the reader questioning the relevance of the theme to their current position within their own lives.

7. Resolutions should not have the feeling of being any of the following: obvious; unbelievable or dull.

8. In the context of the story, resolutions arrived at will probably feel like the only possible answers. In other words, they could have been predicted.

9. Although the reader feels they could have predicted the resolutions, they should not have actually managed to make those predictions.

10. Resolutions will normally involve a surprise of some kind. This is particularly important for the final plot

resolution and the use of a surprise to facilitate resolution will help to leave readers satisfied.

11. Above all, if a plot or sub-plot has no resolution whatsoever, then it is not part of the story. It simply becomes padding, wasted words, the probable outcome of which is reader disillusionment.

Despite the limited space afforded to develop plots, sub-plots or themes within a flash story format, you should still aim to have a plot, a theme, or both. If you are using flash to work on the dynamics of a sub-plot in a much larger story then the sub-plot simply becomes the main plot of your flash. It is worth remembering that, even in stories with a factual base, it is important to identify and develop your main plot and the sub-plots. Just as in purely fictional works, if a true-life plot or sub-plot has no resolution then it too is simply padding. It does not form a true part of the real story which is being told. Using the flash format on sub-plots is likely to highlight if a sub-plot is really part of a bigger story.

In flash fiction we also need resolution. On occasion, we may deliver a complete story resolution even in a flash piece. An example of this is found in the story, The Unhappy Snowman, found in the Quick Fix Flash part of this book. The theme is 'the healing properties of compassion for others'. When the snowman finds he has compassion for others within him he is suddenly healed of his self-centred misery. The snowman's discovery is only possible through the conflict and tension in the story. There can be no resolution without conflict.

Although the snowman story provides an example of complete resolution, the reader is not told if the robin's chicks, off scene in a nest somewhere, survive. In fact, this issue is resolved through the sentiment of the story. It is inconceivable that the chicks would not survive after the sacrifice made by the snowman. Issues can be resolved by implication rather than spelling out every single detail to the reader. It is important to respect the reader's intelligence and allow them to arrive at their own satisfactory conclusions.

When struggles are only partially resolved, as in the case of many flash pieces, the flash story forms the start of a much larger story. Readers will immediately identify the fact that a story is incomplete but, because some issues have been resolved, the reader is able to understand the emotions of the story going forward. In other words, in the brief flash space, you still need to provide readers with the tools they need to make some sense out of the story.

Here is an example of a plot and a theme presented in less than 250 words. The story is incomplete, as are the story's resolutions. We do not know if our main character survives or dies. Neither do we know if he will have faith in God at the end of his ordeal. When reading the example, try separating narrative, thoughts and speech with the objective of identifying what aspects of the lead character's struggles have been partially resolved:

Santa Magdalene's Last

Now the sharks circle, vultures of the sea, smelling death.

How do they know? Three blistering days now, and three frozen nights since the Santa Magdalene sank. I don't understand. Why did God spare me? To scorch and freeze me? Torture me with thirst? Terror me with those cold-blooded killers?

"God help me. Please, God, hear me."

If only my swollen tongue could shout.

"You saved me once. Please, God, save me again."

What am I saying? What in Christ's name...? Countless millions suffering. I'm selfish. Others need Him more.

"Don't waste time on me. Not when others suffer more."

Some poor soul, without strength. I can still fight. I can face death.

"You've helped me once. Do you hear me? Help someone else."

I have my faith. I always have my faith.

*

Sharks circle. Closer now. Vultures. Willing me dead.

How do they know? Four blistering days and four frozen nights. Now I understand. God spared me to torture me with those cold dead eyes.

"What inhuman thing are You?"

He won't hear me. Even if my tongue could shout, He wouldn't help. If He exists? He creates suffering. What sort of God...?

"I don't need you. Do you hear me? Amuse yourself with some other dumb soul."

I won't beg. I won't. I'd rather die.

"You don't exist. Do you hear me? You don't exist."

****

By the end of this story, the only thing that we have learned, in fact the only issue that is partially resolved, is the lead character's courage and determination to fight his fear. This is a problem that is internal but it is brought out by the catastrophic nature of the external event. Whatever happens, our lead will live or die fighting. His reaction to moments of weakness and failure is always to rebound with defiance. Our lead character might end up dying, we don't know, but he certainly won't go quietly. We know this because the story is partially resolved. Whatever happens, our lead will face the insurmountable challenges with defiant bravery, despite his natural human capacity for fear and doubt.

Since the next section is discussing the development of analytical skills you may wish to try a small task before you read the next section. Santa Magdalene's Last is a short flash which could equally be purely fictional or based on fact. With reference to the tools that have been presented so far in this section, try to analyse the story in terms of: imagination; tension and conflict;

character; point of view; dialogue; showing and telling; expectations and resolutions. The exercise should leave you able to make specific comments about the story which go far beyond simply stating whether or not the story is to your taste.

3.9 Analytical Skills

I remember a friend of mine telling me about a time that he took a group of first year undergraduate university students to a local art gallery to study religious iconography. He introduced the group to the first painting to be studied and asked them if they had any initial ideas or comments. As is often true in these circumstances, the students were reluctant to comment at first but then one tentatively put up their hand and said, "I don't like the colour." This resulted in a whole raft of similar comments.

The reason that I tell this story is not to ridicule the students involved. On the contrary, it was their education that was lacking because they had reached a stage in education where they should already have been taught that there is more to understand in a situation than simply your own subjective feelings. It is not that our subjective realities are not important but rather, it is a mistake to teach people that the only thing that matters is their own subjective view. Far too much emphasis had been placed on their subjectivity to the detriment of objectivity. It was almost as though their earlier learning had deliberately subjugated their natural ability to critically analyse.

It is important to make this point because there may be some of you reading this who believe that you are not analytical. Perhaps you think you're a 'feelings' person and therefore cannot make an objective analysis. If you do feel that, it is certain that you were taught to think like that from a very young age. In fact, the objective analysis of any stimulus is the very thing that separates human reasoning from that of other animals. Our natural innate ability to look at a situation, analyse it using our

80

powers of abstraction, and then make a whole raft of suppositions based upon those abstractions is the human faculty that made modern human existence possible. Cognitive reasoning is a feature of our species, not a special ability possessed by just a few privileged individuals. You can critically analyse. We all can.

That established, we now need to look at what we mean by critical analysis but the first thing to highlight is what is not meant. People can sometimes be confused by a narrow definition of the word 'critical' and this leads them to believe that critical analysis is negative. It is not. In making a critical analysis. it is equally important to identify those features that it would be extremely difficult to improve. In fact, identifying what is working in any situation helps humans to replicate successful strategies without recourse to constant failure. Practising to do something badly only makes a person good at doing something badly. Just like every other skill, critical analysis is something that can be practised. However, it does require that we, as individuals, give the same weight of importance to our critical understanding as we do to our subjective responses.

To achieve this, it is helpful to see critical analysis as the process by which we identify three crucial things:

1. Firstly, those things that we do not need to tamper with because they are already working pretty much as we intended (note: I did not say perfectly because we assume perfection not to be a human trait but seeing what is good is just as much a part of any critical analysis as identifying what does not work);

2. Secondly, those things that need immediate attention because they are not fulfilling the purpose for which they were intended (these are the parts that are not working at all, or are serving absolutely no purpose within the story);

3. Finally, those things that work to an extent, could use some improvement and must be addressed, but only after

the major problems have been corrected or generally improved (these parts of a story may work better without further attention once the major problems have been addressed).

For many readers of this book, this will all feel obvious but that is not a bad thing. It means that we are in a position to go forward, some readers with a new found confidence. We can critically analyse both our own work, and the work of others, in order to improve our writing skills. This is achieved by using the guidelines on writing, presented in this book, to systematically analyse how the application of these guidelines can improve the stories that we encounter.

This section has shown critical analysis to be a useful skill that everyone has the innate ability to learn and improve. With such appreciation, we are in a position to wield critical analysis as a tool to improve our own writing. Flash fiction is particularly useful in this regard. Extremely short stories provide a compact scope of application which means we can more easily apply guidelines to focus our critical analysis. It provides a forum where we can use our learning to identify and specify areas, in the execution of a piece of writing, from sublime grace to clumsy meaninglessness. Through this process of critical analysis, we develop our ability as writers.

3.10 Technical

In line with the rest of this toolkit, this section provides a general discussion of a number of technical issues, rather than spelling out the minutiae of how to write well technically. In fact, sometimes creative writing will involve bending, or even breaking technical rules, for example, rules on sentence construction. Nevertheless, it is important for less experienced writers to take just as much care and consideration over how and when they bend the rules, as do more established writers.

There are many technical books on grammar, punctuation and sentence construction and no purpose would be served by repetition here. However, when a writer wishes to create a dramatic effect, the semantic content is only one key factor that needs to be considered. Another major factor, which is equally important, particularly when attempting to invoke an emotional reaction from the reader, is the use of language structure. This structure is controlled by the writer's manipulation of sentences using punctuation and grammar. For example, a writer wishing to increase pace and tension may do so by the staccato delivery of short, unpunctuated or even ungrammatical sentences. A feeling of calmness, on the other hand, may be enhanced by long drifting sentences making extensive use of punctuation to keep the reader in tune with the flow of idea.

Earlier in this book we briefly looked at the issues of closeness and empathy in relation to the point of views used to tell a story. Just like point of view, the tense too can have a major impact on the reader's ability to empathise with characters. Using the present tense increases closeness, whilst using the past tense injects some distance. However, past tense is extremely useful, particularly for the aspiring writer, because it can be easier to execute. As a result, when writing in past tense, the starting out writer is far less likely to become confused, start switching tenses and, as a result, make a complete hash of their story.

The question of which tense to use for your story can create a degree of uncertainty. For this reason many starting-out writers opt for the simplest option by using past tense in conjunction with third person point of view. Care still needs to be taken to stay consistent in the narrative voice, because people speak to each other in the present tense, and so all dialogue must be in present tense even when the speech tags are indicating that the conversation took place in the past. For example:

Dr Goodbody felt for Suzie's pulse,

"How are you feeling today?"

In this example, the character is speaking in present tense whilst the action and speech tag (narrator voice) is clearly in the past. It is important, particularly when there is a lot of dialogue and very little narration, that the narrative voice does not make accidental present tense slips.

It can be even more challenging when opting for other tense/point of view combinations. As already alluded to, the benefit of present tense/first person point of view is the increased closeness to both the characters and the action. However, staying entirely in the present takes an enormous effort if the narrative delivered by the point of view character, rather than an omniscient narrator, is to feel genuine. Even in the hands of an established writer, this combination can feel awkward to read. Attempting this strategy in a memoir can be even more of a challenge because you are telling a story about events that actually happened to you, the writer, at some time in the past, so there is always a great temptation to slip back into the past tense.

Using the flash format, where you can really focus down on the tense and point of view combination, allows experimentation and facilitates learning. The writer of a flash piece can rapidly spot any errors in the tense and point of view combination which often means that the cause of the slip can also be identified.

When preparing a larger work, using flash for scene development can greatly assist the writer in making their tense and point of view choices. Finding out that you have made the wrong choice for the tense and point of view combination, when already 40,000 words into the writing a full-scale story, can be sickening. A thorough investigation of your key scenes and action sequences using flash will help to ensure that the choice, made at the start, really is the best one for you and your story.

3.11 Diktats

Yes, I know what I said about rules but these diktats are really only suggestions too. However, in the end, I couldn't resist listing a few rules for my own entertainment. In the main, these rules are quotations from The Guardian's ten rules for writing fiction. This was produced from a survey of established authors, conducted by The Guardian, to elicit tips for successful authorship. The Guardian gives credit for their inspiration to Elmore Leonard's book, 10 Rules of Writing. You can find all the tips in the aforementioned Guardian article but here are some quotes to whet your appetite. The titles are mine but the quotes belong to the referenced authors.

1. Elmore Leonard defines mortal sin:
Never use an adverb to modify the verb "said" ... he admonished gravely. To use an adverb this way (or almost any way) is a mortal sin. The writer is now exposing himself in earnest, using a word that distracts and can interrupt the rhythm of the exchange. I have a character in one of my books tell how she used to write historical romances "full of rape and adverbs".

2. Roddy Doyle defines risky behaviour:
Do not place a photograph of your favourite author on your desk, especially if the author is one of the famous ones who committed suicide.

3. Geoff Dyer defines toileting:
Don't write in public places. In the early 1990s I went to live in Paris. The usual writerly reasons: back then, if you were caught writing in a pub in England, you could get your head kicked in, whereas in Paris, dans les cafés . . . Since then I've developed an aversion to writing in public. I now think it should be done only in private, like any other lavatorial activity.

4. Anne Enright defines life and death:
Imagine that you are dying. If you had a terminal disease

would you finish this book? Why not? The thing that annoys this 10-weeks-to-live self is the thing that is wrong with the book. So change it. Stop arguing with yourself. Change it. See? Easy. And no one had to die.

5. Richard Ford defines:
I like Ford's rules but including them all here would constitute a copy rather than a quote so I need to direct you to see if you can find Ford's original rules in the Guardian's list, or you might find them on the internet.

6. Jonathan Franzen defines fact as fiction:
The most purely autobiographical fiction requires pure invention. Nobody ever wrote a more auto biographical story than "The Metamorphosis".

7. Neil Gaiman defines finished:
Remember that, sooner or later, before it ever reaches perfection, you will have to let it go and move on and start to write the next thing. Perfection is like chasing the horizon. Keep moving.

8. A.L Kennedy defines your limits:
Remember you don't know the limits of your own abilities. Successful or not, if you keep pushing beyond yourself, you will enrich your own life – and maybe even please a few strangers.

9. Hilary Mantel defines bad influences:
If you get stuck, get away from your desk. Take a walk, take a bath, go to sleep, make a pie, draw, listen to music, meditate, exercise; whatever you do, don't just stick there scowling at the problem. But don't make telephone calls or go to a party; if you do, other people's words will pour in where your lost words should be. Open a gap for them, create a space. Be patient.

10. Michael Moorcock defines your rules:
Ignore all proffered rules and create your own, suitable for what you want to say.

11. Michael Morpurgo defines being fortunate:
Once the skeleton of the story is ready I begin talking about it, mostly to Clare, my wife, sounding her out.

12. Will Self defines the book not to write:
Live life and write about life. Of the making of many books there is indeed no end, but there are more than enough books about books.

13. Colm Tóibín defines success:
Finish everything you start.

14. Rose Tremain defines enhancing understanding:
Forget the boring old dictum "write about what you know". Instead, seek out an unknown yet knowable area of experience that's going to enhance your understanding of the world and write about that.

15 Sarah Waters defines an approach to the works of others:
Read like mad. But try to do it analytically – which can be hard, because the better and more compelling a novel is, the less conscious you will be of its devices. It's worth trying to figure those devices out, however: they might come in useful in your own work. I find watching films also instructive. Nearly every modern Hollywood blockbuster is hopelessly long and baggy. Trying to visualise the much better films they would have been with a few radical cuts is a great exercise in the art of storytelling.

Finally, if the Guardian had asked me for my rules of writing anything, either fact-based or purely fictional, I would certainly have included some rules which link directly back to the very beginning of this book. It was there that we first mentioned the importance of ensuring that you share the story that you have inside you. You can only have the possibility to succeed if you commit to action. I don't wish to trawl all my ideas in order to then pervert them into rules. However, I don't mind telling you a few things that I try to keep telling myself. These are little messages rather than rules and regardless of how hard I try, I can become so discouraged that I lose my grip on my own messages to myself. Anyway, here are a few of those messages:

1. Set times to get the story out because later is never now.

2. Don't take the comments of rude and arrogant (or stupid) people to heart.

3. Try to spot and combat arrogance and stupidity in yourself.

4. Strive to be open to constructive criticism.

5. Try to be the best you can even if you don't feel that you have natural talent.

6. The real battle is with yourself, not a competition between you and others, despite what others might say.

7. Paranoia does not protect ideas, it stifles them.

8. Don't worry when a good idea is lost because if one is possible then more are too.

9. You don't need to make up additional rules just to make lists reach some arbitrary number that seems significant based upon your past experience.

4. Final thoughts

Numerous writers have used the flash fiction format for a wide range of purposes. No doubt, similar forms of writing have always been used as an approach to scene development or specification, even if sometimes writers are not aware that this is what they are doing. Such writing uses the discrete nature of flash to create standalone pieces which nevertheless, fit directly into the writers overall plot for a larger work.

The flash method also allows writers to ensure that scenes or events make sense in their own right. Tension almost forces itself into the first beats of a flash piece and makes each scene one from which the reader will find it difficult to escape. The writer can rapidly assess the efficacy of a scene and hone both style and content to ensure their goals for the scene are achieved.

In isolation, flash cannot be used to tackle larger factual or fictional works. Here, the writer is required to organise and martial story events such that the reader is pulled along inside the story. One way of achieving this is through the creation of story maps which keep the writer on track with regards to connectivity between story events. Using a combination of flash and story mapping, an aspiring writer can develop their skills and then use those skills to move beyond the start of their next large work and go right through to actual completion

4.1 Story maps

One of the real beauties of flash writing, for someone just starting out on their writing journey, is that the scale of work does not require any real forward planning. In fact, it would be highly unusual for a writer to try to plan a flash piece. Flash works tend to be organic and simply develop as they are written. However, the same cannot always be said of larger works. When tackling extensive writing challenges, mapping ideas can prove extremely useful.

Story mapping may not be the solution for everyone but it may be useful to see if the technique is one which suites you. For those who are aspiring to write their first larger piece, or for those who have made numerous false starts, maps can be particularly useful.

There are many starting-out writers who have managed to write reams without ever having completed any of those embryonic stories. The reason for this is often a loss of direction at some mid-point. When a writer does not know where to go next it becomes extremely difficult to continue and this can result in repeated false starts. Even worse, it is possible to reach a mid-point and realise that the story has nowhere to go.

Numerous books detail a wide variety of methods for writing plots. When starting out, I must admit, I did read a great number of such books and I did try to implement the systems that they proposed. Whichever system I tried, the result was the same; failure. It is only once a certain level of skill has been developed that such systems become useable. Even then, I found such systems boring and damaging to my creative energy.

A further problem is that such plotting methods are specifically designed for fictional writing. There is no discussion of fact-based works such as biographies and memoirs. Yet factual stories are equally in need of tools to facilitate their creation. Just because something happened in real-life does not mean that it can simply be written down. The story still needs to be told. The plot still needs to be crafted.

However, there is an important point being made in all those story planning books. The important point they make is that planning can, for some writers, be extremely helpful. A writing plan is a kind of map that you can follow when things get tough. You can choose where a journey starts, where it ends, and the route that the journey will follow. However, unlike plotting systems, which promote high levels of detail and completeness, the type of story map that I would like to propose does not require extensive detail. It is quick and simple to create, it can be viewed at a glance, and it can also be modified in just a few seconds. For the starting out writer, these features are extremely useful and help the writer maintain their direction whilst creating a larger piece of work.

Unlike a traditional map, a story map is not set in stone. There are no defined places and no roads. In fact, even when the map has been created it will not look like a map, but rather, it will take the form of a multi-level list. This book was mapped using this mapping technique and I have deliberately left the basic structure of the story embedded within the final work. You can see the list of lists in the chapter titles with each chapter being formed from sub-sections. Of course, this is a factual book and the technique is drawn from that genre. However, there is absolutely no reason that the same technique cannot be applied to fictional work. The important point to understand is that each heading in a list of lists story map can have as much, or as little, detail as you require in order for you to remember the embryonic idea referred to by the heading.

Many writers will say that the most important part of writing is the creation of strong and interesting characters. This is because all stories are character driven. However, this assertion suggests that stories begin with characters and then stories naturally fall from those characters. While this is partly true, when presented in this way it leads starting out writers into a position where they are likely to create many starts to stories but never any completed works. Without a story, even strong characters don't know what to do next. The writer needs events for their strong characters and it is the events, not the characters, which form the story map.

Construction of the initial map is quick and easy. You may not have a fully formed idea of your story but the fact that you are thinking of writing a story means that you probably have some idea of at least some of the events that will occur in your story. The initial map is a list of those events. At this point there should be no detail attached to the list. It is simply a list of the major events. Try to place the list of events in the order that you would like the reader to be made aware of them when you are telling your story. Notice, this is not necessarily the order in which the events occur. If any additional events come to mind or are suggested by the re-ordering process then add those to your list in the appropriate place in the telling of your story. You now have an embryonic story map.

Look at the map and check it for completeness. It will certainly not be complete but checking it at this stage will often allow you to locate areas where events are missing. Such events may even be crucial parts of your story such as the beginning and the ending. In fact, in my experience, the true beginning will emerge only once a reasonable part of the story has already been written. In addition, even when you have a good idea of how your story ends, it is highly likely that the ending will not be exactly how you thought it would be when you first started committing the story to prose.

The next stage of creating the story map involves working with your embryonic list of major story events. For each event on the list, write another list of the event's constituent parts. For example: you have a major event where your lead character loses her wedding ring. This could easily precipitate or indicate a major part of any story, factual or fictional. What were the small events that surrounded the losing of the ring? There were reasons why the ring fell off or was removed. There was a series of circumstances that led to the ring being lost. Write this list under your scene heading and do this for every major event in your story. You now have a fully fledged story map.

The story map you create will neither be complete nor correct but it will outline your initial story idea. It is simple, easy to read and can be modified extremely quickly. As you are writing your story you will constantly develop and refer to your story map. When you don't know where you are going refer back to the story map. Major events become chapters and sub-events provide the story fragments that can be explored and developed using the flash fiction method. Each sub-event can be studied and worked upon as a stand-alone flash so that the sheer scale of a larger work is never over-whelming.

For some people, story maps can also deal with the problem of becoming blocked or stagnant. Since the document map releases the writer from the serial execution of their story, there should never be a time when the writer cannot contribute to the writing of their story. Even if you are a writer who prefers to write a story in a strictly linear fashion, the act of jumping briefly to another scene could prove liberating.

When faced with a difficult section, or one that is proving challenging, the writer simply scans the list of lists for something else they would like to write about and start developing flashes of those sub-events. In this way, if you do suffer from writer's block, this technique can very often unblock you, and reinvigorate your positive emotions towards completing the larger work. Through turning a large task into many small and easily achievable tasks, the large task itself will become more achievable.

A story map is never incorrect, but rather, it is simply that story maps are always subject to constant modification and revision. This is a natural feature of the writer's development of story ideas. The story map develops in parallel with these ideas and will only be completed when the larger story is itself completely written. The map is subject to continuous scrutiny, deletions, additions, modifications and reorganisation. However, such revisions become a simple matter of picking up entire sections, themselves made of a list of lists, and dropping them into a new location in the high level list. In this way, all the relevant story pieces stick together and help the writer to modify the telling of their story in seconds. This allows the story map to serve as a constant guide throughout the entire writing process. Since the map is never set in stone, a quick reorganisation can often solve problems that might otherwise lead to an abandoned work.

4.2 Factual flash and creativity

As I have already stated, short story forms such as flash, are equally appropriate for fact-based works, memoirs and biographies. In fact, this book, which is essentially a factual book, was entirely written using a flash-like format in that each sub-section was separately created as a word-limited stand-alone piece. Sub-sections were created sequentially when my flow allowed but, whenever I became blocked I simply jumped to a different sub-section and tackled that instead.

The story map provides the glue that holds the book together as a whole story. The order of the final book is defined, modified and redesigned using the document map. Even this late on in writing this book I have just removed a chapter and turned it into a sub-section using the story map. This allowed me to address an issue of balance within the book in a simple and efficient way.

Memoirs and biographies stand somewhere between a factual book, such as this one, and a purely fictional story book. There is little room for characterisation in a book such as this but story is still the key. Even this book must tell a story. In memoirs and biographies, there is plenty of room for characterisation. The writer may not have quite the level of overall freedom that is available in a purely fictional work, but the scope for character development is still there even if it is guided by true life events. Facts are interpreted and as such, even factual stories are always, at least in part, fiction.

In the context of Write with Flash, I made a general guide for the length of a flash piece at below 2000 words. Obviously, anyone can play around with formats but those limits do provide a useful starting point for both flash fiction and factual flash. Such limits provide ample space for the development of story ideas even if such limits may need to be extended in many cases. Engaging in brevity can be instructional when trying to develop a strong writing style for use in longer works.

Repeatedly, throughout this book, I have highlighted the creative nature of fact-based writing. It is not the poor relative of fictional work, nor does it take any less imagination when executed well. Both factual and fictional stories require tremendous imagination and commitment from the writer to bring those stories to readers in a form which grips them and keeps them reading all the way to the end.

It may be true that, in years past, fact-based writing in the form of non-celebrity biographies and memoirs were more popular. Today, they are well off the popularity levels that they enjoyed in their heyday. Nevertheless, if the first story that you wish to tell happens to be non-celebrity biographical, you should not let that discourage you. Once you have written your first larger work, you may well be inspired to develop your writing further and try other types of writing. That book that you feel is in you could well be just the first of many.

4.3 Quality

I am advocating that anyone who feels they have a story to tell also has the right to have a go at recording and sharing them. Since this is so, then it is also important that I address the question of quality. It is not sufficient for anyone to simply write down a whole bunch of words and call those words a story. Again, at the risk of being accused of cliché, if a story is worth telling then it is worth telling well. Our stories are worth our very best efforts and that means two things:

1. We need to continue to educate ourselves throughout our writing endeavours, so that we are able to understand how to turn the thoughts in our heads into a form where our written words will effect a change, a kind of growth, in the people who read them.

2. We need to accept that our first effort is unlikely to be our best effort. This means that the first draft of any story that we write will only ever be a draft. It is a start but that is all it is. After creating the first draft, we all need to review our efforts and revise them. Review, revise and review again until we are ready to share our efforts with someone else who is also willing and able to critically review our efforts.

Only after we have submitted to these processes is it likely that our efforts will be of a reasonable standard. At that point, we are then in a position to share our work with other people more generally and have some hope that they will be able to benefit from reading our stories. In the final analysis, it is the impact that our writing has on our readers lives which determines the success, or otherwise, of our writing efforts.

4.4 Exercise

I have deliberately used the imperative form, 'Exercise' as the heading for this section. If you want to get fit then you must exercise but you choose the exercises that are most appropriate for you. It is the same with writing. If you wish to improve your writing then you need to exercise. Again, it is up to you to choose the exercises which will be most useful to you and your current level of development.

Almost everyone reading this book will have encountered exercises and tasks for writers. These are used to: hone the writer's existing skills through practise; introduce and develop new skills; and also break down any blockages to writing that may be stultifying the writer.

The main danger when encountering exercises is that, without a structured class, which creates an imperative beyond the writers own personal development, exercises are skim-read and never undertaken. The same is true of this book. Where exercises are indicated, they can only be effectual if they are actually undertaken.

For the aforementioned reasons, rather than specify a large set of tasks and writing exercises, I have decided to provide a general approach which is directly related to the content of this book. The exercises are self-directed and address: developing critical analysis; mapping stories; and flashing the scenes from much larger stories. More simply, these techniques can be referred to as critiquing, mapping and flashing.

a) Critiquing

A useful way to improve critical analysis can be undertaken by the simple application of the 'Write with Flash Toolkit' to the stories presented in 'Quick Fix Fiction'. This is particularly useful because the stories in this book are of the flash format and can, therefore, be analysed far more rapidly than trying to undertake the same task using full scale novels, biographies or memoirs.

There are two key ways in which such analysis can be attempted, either with the focus on a particular tool or with the focus on a particular story. There is no correct choice. It is simply down to how you feel like addressing the task at the time. As a person who is constantly striving to understand more fully the process of storytelling myself, I often try to analyse the films that I watch and the books that I read with a critical eye on how the story is delivered. For me, studying the work of others in this way has proved a tremendous learning experience and continues to do so.

A tool-based approach is most useful for very short pieces, such as the flash stories presented in this book. Here, you take any single guideline from the toolkit and apply it to the stories. For example, you might decide you wish to focus on dialogue. If so, you would then read several stories, perhaps at random and apply what you understand about dialogue to those stories. It should be possible to identify if the dialogue is naturalistic, purposeful and engaging. You can also inspect technical issues such as any speech tags or associated action tags. This should allow you to work out how you would approach the dialogue in a similar situation, story or scene.

The story-based approach can also be used on the flash pieces in this book but here we take everything that we generally understand about the delivery of stories and apply it to one story in particular. In this way, we would critically assess a single story against the criteria set out here and identify the places where the storytelling works really well and the places where it seems to fall down. By comparing a story with the guidelines in this, and other toolkits, we can start to see the techniques that are being used and the relative success with which they have been executed. Again, this provides an ideal opportunity to start thinking how we, as writers, might do things differently.

The story-based approach is also extremely useful when we are simply enjoying films or books. In these circumstances, our critically tuned thought processes can operate at a level just below consciousness so that, periodically, we become consciously aware of the successes and limitations in the works of others.

b) Mapping

People who decide to try the mapping approach outlined in this book may immediately wish to apply it to their own story ideas. Whilst this may intuitively seem like the best way to practise the technique, it may prove more instructive to think about a story you know well, it could be a film or a book, and attempt to recall the story in the form of a list of lists. I think a film is probably the best form with which to experiment initially because it takes very little time to review the film and check how well, or otherwise, we have managed to map the story. It is then possible to modify the story map to correct errors and fill-in any missing details.

Practising in this way, will not only help with developing story-mapping skills, but will also highlight the twists and turns in stories that have some commercial success. This is not to say that commercial success is necessarily your aim, however, such success is one measure of a work's general appeal. Understanding the structure of successful works can be used in the analysis of your own story maps, even when you do not wish to implement the identified strategies. The application of the technique to the stories written by others will almost certainly make it easier to execute story mapping in the context of your own work.

If you do decide to apply the story mapping technique to your own work, it is useful to keep in mind that a story map is never complete until you arrive at the end of your finished story. When a block is encountered, rather than trying to retrace your steps to find where you may have strayed, simply return to the story map. Look through the list of lists which form the map and see if there is a heading for which you feel you could write a flash. You are not losing your story by working at some random point within it. What is actually happening is the clarification of yet another one of the blanks. Persevere, and eventually there will be no blanks left to address and the first draft of your story will be complete.

I find it best not to sit and fiddle with the story map. Here I am making a distinction between fiddling and revising. Fiddling involves playing with the story map when you are feeling bored or uninspired. In such circumstances, it can be tempting to fiddle with the story map rather than finding another section for which to flash out a few ideas. The problem is that any changes made to the story map, due to lack of inspiration, will themselves be uninspired. As a result, it is very likely that the story map will simply become confused.

Instead, I find it far better to only make changes to story maps when those changes are inspired. I will usually encounter either an issue in the story flow or a new idea for story flow whilst writing at full tilt. At these times, I know that the idea for revising the story map is inspired and I usually place a double hash, followed by a couple of words to remind me of the change to the story map, right there in the middle of my work. Then, when I have finished writing, I scan back through the work to find my double hash tag and transport it over into my story map. The revision of the story map is then insightful, purposeful and even obvious. There is no fiddling, just directed revision.

c) Flashing

The flash fiction format is highly attractive when applied as a tool for self training, experimentation, story development and even for the execution of discrete sections to be fed into larger works. This makes flash sound like a panacea to solve all writing problems, which obviously it is not. It is, however, a tool that I am using myself to assist my own life-long learning.

In addition, we all have our limitations: social; psychological; or physical. For many people, such limitations act as blocks to prevent them from achieving their ambitions. With people who feel that they have stories in them that they would like to express in book form, individual limitations often form blocks which prevent them from ever achieving their writing aims. Through the use of the flash writing format, I have found that writing tasks, which can feel overwhelming in scale, become a series of small and easily achievable tasks. It is a method which can help people to overcome their limitations and achieve, in some cases, their lifetime ambition.

From a self training perspective, one technique, which is particularly useful in the context of this book, is to rewrite some of the stories presented in 'Quick Fix Flash'. Some of the guidelines may be appropriate for your versions of the stories and it is possible to experiment with their application. Such a strategy can make a writer fluent in applying their previous knowledge of writing in their first draft attempts. As a result, it is possible to become more aware of exactly what we wish to achieve, so that when we go back to read over what we have written, it is more likely that we have met our objectives, even when we had not consciously formulated those objectives at the outset.

I have already addressed the use of flash for larger works and the way that it can be used in conjunction with story mapping. However, I would like to stress the idea of experimentation. Since flash is discrete, it is possible to experiment with multiple solutions for any story idea. This is far from wasted effort as, in addition to helping in the search for the best way to deliver a story idea, it also provides a further opportunity to exercise your writing skills. This really amounts to writing exercise. The more practise, the greater likelihood of improvement. When working on a larger work, the writer does not need to be satisfied with their first effort and, if using the flash approach, there is no great difficulty experimenting with multiple ideas.

4.5 Conclusion

Throughout, I have held the following ambitions for this book:

1. To provide encouragement. Literally, to give courage to anyone who needs a little help to write their story. Such encouragement is not dependent upon a person's psychological, social and physical attributes or limitations. Everyone is entitled to try to achieve the best that they can achieve and share their achievements with others.

2. To demonstrate that many basic characteristics of storytelling can be applied to any story, whether fact-based or purely fictional. The books that aspiring writers feel they have in them may be of limited commercial appeal but, even when that is the case, that should not be the reason for them not to write their story.

3. To provide a set of tools for aspiring writers regardless of the genre in which they wish to write. The ideas presented in this book are deliberately general so that discrete parts of the book can be chosen and used, or rejected and discarded, at will. The aim is for all of the ideas presented in this book to have the potential for practical application.

4. To show how advice on writing fiction, obtained from any source, is often applicable to the writing of fact-based stories. This helps us to think creatively about using advice on fiction writing, where applicable, to develop fact-based stories.

5. To highlight the importance of critical analysis for our own development as writers. Critical analysis is not a criticism of a work but rather, it is an analysis of a piece of work using our natural critical faculties, in tandem with personal experience and training, to interpret and communicate accurately and effectively with regard to a work's qualities and features. Critical analysis should not undermine, but should be a support for our work and for the work of others. There is nothing to be gained from insulting others and it is probably not the healthiest position to see ourselves in conflict with other writers. Receive constructive critical analysis with interest and appreciation and likewise, strive to be constructive.

7. To identify flash as a format for aspiring writers to use when self training, experimental writing and scene development for larger works. Critiquing, mapping and

flashing can provide the tools for aspiring writers to create completed works of which they can be rightly proud.

In the final analysis, I hope that you, as that most important person in the context of this book, the reader, have found this to be a useful support to your writing ambitions. Without doubt, there are many further steps that we all must take, and there are many resources 'out there' created by some, who may be far more knowledgeable than me. Nevertheless, I do hope that this book has helped to fill a gap between books on basic writing skills and those aimed at people who already have a well-developed understanding of how to achieve their writing goals. I wish you courage and strength as you now set out to write your stories.

5. Quick Fix Flash

Quick Fix Flash provides a series of stories, partly for your entertainment but also for use in conjunction with the toolkit presented earlier in this book.

Some readers, particularly those who find they deal with instructional material best in short bursts, may have flicked to this section without already completing the earlier chapters. If so, I can understand that. Most of us need a break when we are working hard and relaxing with a coffee and a short story is sometimes just the quick fix that we need.

Hopefully, you also intend to use the Write with Flash toolkit to analyse each story. Since flash stories are short, they facilitate such analysis. You may also like to rewrite the stores using what you have learned and their brevity should enable you to execute relatively quick fixes.

Regardless of whether you read the stories for entertainment, or read them to develop your critical understanding, the idea of a quick fix certainly fits.

These stories are toys to read, dismantle, criticise, rewrite or analyse for your own education or enjoyment. By applying the toolkit to these short stories, I hope that you are able to further develop your goal of shining in the art of storytelling.

5.1 A borrower of the night

Title: A borrower of the night
Stimulus: A borrower of the night
Word count: 706

"This is the life eh Pam. I can tell you, retirement definitely suites me, especially when the weather's this good. There's nothing like relaxing with a nice cup of coffee before starting the day. We never had the time to do this when we were working, did we?"

A sharp rap on the door, three hard knocks in quick succession. I tut, lowering my newspaper to grimace at Pam.

"Who the hell is that at this time of the morning? Be a sweetheart and tell them, whatever it is they're selling - we don't want it."

I have to admit it, she is good to me but moving towards the door she can't help sniping at me.

"You're closer. You could try getting up off your lazy backside once in a while."

I'm sure she doesn't really mind. After all the years we've been together it's just become our way.

Cocking my head towards the hallway I hear the door open. Pam's gentle tones make their way back to me but I detect something odd in her voice. I hate my privacy being disturbed by cold callers. Even the sticker in the front window explicitly stating 'we don't buy on the doorstep' doesn't stop the most aggressive sellers. Without doubt, this is just such a salesman.

And it's definitely a salesman rather than a saleswoman. It's a man's voice I can hear. Straining my ears, I can't quite work out what's being said, but he does sound formal. My curiosity is piqued.

Considering leaning my chair back, I could twist my head and catch a glimpse of the intruder. But I'm not quite that curious. Slumping lazily, I settle, back to my repose. Hearing the bang of the door as it closes completes my relief.

"Jim."

"Yes love."

"It's the police. They want to talk to you."

Tipping back and twisting to look at Pam I nearly fall of my seat. There, standing just behind her, is a tall policeman, his dark uniform highlighting his power and authority.

"What is it? What's happened?"

Shock grips my body. Blood rises in my head and pounds through my inner ears, flushing red as though guilty of something, though I don't know what.

"Mr. James Patterson?"

"Yes. Is there something wrong?"

"You are the registered keeper of a black Toyota Avensis registration number PL08 FGD?"

"Yes. That's right."

"Have you loaned your vehicle to anyone, or to your knowledge, has anyone borrowed your vehicle within the last 12 hours."

"No. It's been in the drive all night. It hasn't been stolen, has it?"

A tremendous sinking feeling pulls my heart down to my stomach.

"Stolen." My head sways involuntarily. Shocked by my own words, like a burst balloon, instantly and utterly deflated.

"No Sir. Your car is still in the driveway...", half relief clashes with confusion, "and so how do you explain the extensive damage to the front of your vehicle?"

"What damage? My car isn't damaged."

"Good try Sir. - James Patterson, I am arresting you on suspicion of being involved in a hit and run accident. You do not have to say anything. But it may harm your defence if you do not mention when questioned something which you later rely on in court. Anything you do say may be given in evidence."

Stunned. I try to move but, where there was bone and muscle just a moment ago, only jelly remains.

Seeking refuge from the swirling turmoil I turn to Pam. Her look of mute fear stuns me to blind panic.

108

"It's some crazy mistake. Tell him Pam. I didn't do it. Someone must have taken my car."

Every last feature of Pam's face is frozen, petrified in horror.

The policeman smiles, "And then brought it back again I suppose?"

He grips my forearm, powerfully pulling me to my feet.

"Are you going to come of your own free will, or do I need to cuff you."

"Pam. Pam. For God's sake. I'm innocent. Tell him. I'm innocent"

The policeman guides me towards the door but I manage to twist, desperate to snatch a final reassuring glance at Pam.

I see a flash of something. Is it a smirk? Instantly it's gone and her face flushes.

Oh my God. Pam?

5.2 The unhappy snowman

Title: The unhappy snowman
Stimulus: A Christmas card image of a snow scene with a robin and a snowman.
Word count: 781

"What are you chirping about?"

Snowman tried to frown at Robin but found his features frozen on his face.

"I can't see what you're so happy about."

"Sorry," said Robin, "I didn't mean to disturb you. I can't help chirping. It's my nature. It's just what Robins do."

"Well, it's irritating," said Snowman trying to wave his arms to frighten Robin but immediately noticed that he had no arms to wave."

"Look," said Robin, "I wasn't doing anyone any harm and you just started growling at me for no reason."

"No reason," snapped Snowman. "No reason? Of course I've got a reason. And if you took a moment to think about others rather than just smugly chirping about how happy you are then it would be obvious to you why I am so unhappy."

Robin paused for a moment and took a long hard look at Snowman.

"Well," said Robin, "I've taken a moment to look and what stands out most is that you have a lovely big smile on your face."

"Just because a person is smiling, it doesn't necessarily mean that they are happy," said Snowman. "When the children built me they made me have this smiling face. Now there is nothing I can do about it but it doesn't mean that I am happy."

"I'm very sorry about that," said Robin, who was confused as to how anyone could possibly be unhappy about smiling.

"It's like this," said Snowman, "you don't notice other people's problems because you don't really have any. You can keep warm by fluttering about and happily chirping while I'm stuck here freezing cold. I can't even waggle my toes because I don't have any. I can't go anywhere, or even turn around to see what's behind me. I can't do anything except sit here, unhappily smiling. That's a snowman's lot. I can't even enjoy the sunshine because I know that will make me melt."

"You're too busy thinking about yourself," explained Robin. "Do you really think that nobody else has any problems?"

Snowman snorted, "Well Robin, if everyone has problems then what problems could you possibly have? How can you have problems with your pretty feathers to keep you warm and your wings to effortlessly carry you to wherever you would like to go?"

"Just because you can't see my problems, it doesn't mean that they don't exist" said Robin. "But I really don't wish to burden you with my problems. You seem to have plenty of problems of your own to worry about."

"No," insisted Snowman. "You can't get out of it that easily. How do I know that you really have problems?"

"It's sad that you only want to know about my problems to prove that you have worse problems than me. You aren't really interested in my difficulties. You don't want to help me, or even sympathise with me. I don't really want to talk about my problems but I will because I think that it might help you. I have a little chick at home. She was born early and now the snow has fallen she is cold and hungry. The snow has hidden all the food and so I can't find anything for her to eat. I am so worried. I must find food for her but I cannot go out for very long to look for food because I need to get back to keep her warm."

"Oh, my dear," said Snowman. "I didn't realise. I have wasted your time on my problems when you have such difficult problems of your own. I wish that I could think of some way to help."

"The only thing that will help me is if the sun starts to shine. Then my chick will be warm, the snow will melt and I will be able to find some food for her. But now I have met you I feel so sorry that I am praying for the sunshine to save my chick, but that same sunshine will be the end of you."

112

Snowman noticed a small tear forming in the corner of Robin's eye.

"Don't cry," said Snowman. "I've thought of a way that I can help. Why don't you take my carrot nose to feed your chick until the sun starts to shine again."

"Thank you Snowman", said Robin "but what about you? When the sun starts shining you will melt away."

"Yes, that's true", said Snowman, "but I will be happy because now I know that the sunshine will give life to your chick. You have given me more than you can ever know. You have given me a way to melt happy and that is the greatest gift of all."

5.3 Park life

Title: Park life
Stimulus: Story based on the following character description:
Man intermediate age; Good but old clothes, handmade suits and
shoes leather; Fallen on hard times; Tall, thick mane of white hair
once black; Seems unhappy/ unwell; Travels on buses or walks
everywhere; Tea towel wrapped around one foot, limps.
Word count: 580

Ensuring my gaze never lingers too long in any one direction, a
failing which could easily alert any less than innocent eyes, I
survey the scene in front of me. All the time I bend my ears to
any activity not covered by my vision. The fine weather is a
double edged sword. More people than usual in the park.

Group, four males, early teens, on bikes, street clothes, circling
120 metres distant, executing stunts. Disregard.

Female, entering by south gate, early thirties, overweight, jeans
and T, dog, collie-lab cross, dog alert to female, highly trained.
Disregard.

Two men. Late 40's early 50's, sharp dress, determined gait,
heading west, distance 200 metres, not speaking. Something
suspicious but no immediate threat. Observe.

Approaching steps, from my left, on footpath, male. Threat.
No reaction, no novice errors. Bend peripheral vision to subject.
Tall, athletic, threat. Body on alert. Footsteps slowing, threat.

Subject moves to the bench beside me. Fingers curl slowly
around the blade. No sudden movements. Muscles tense for the
strike. If this is one of them, I will know any second. Careful.
Mustn't kill a civvy. Not on my first deep cover mission.

"Paul."

He knows my codename. One of theirs? One of ours? Don't
be hasty.

"Paul, HQ want you in."

Ah, one of ours.

"You want to be careful coming up on my blind side. Any
sudden movement and you would have had a blade in your face."

"Cut the dramatics Paul. It's over. They want you in. What a bloody mess. You were supposed to be undercover you idiot."

I finally look at the tall man beside me. I don't recognise him but I know his sort. Career professional. Probably never been on the cutting edge like I am. Dangerous all the same. More dangerous than any scumbag gangbanger.

His sort. Order a man dead as soon as draw breath. No need to soil his hands. Send a man like that for me and they mean business.

"Have I been scoped."

"Scoped? Scoped? You damned fool. You're supposed to be incog-bloody-nito not some celebrity sodding hobo. Why couldn't you just have been some homeless guy that no-one takes a second glance at. You're a bloody parody. Only a blind man in a hurry wouldn't SCOPE you."

He's ridiculing me. Snide git. Wish he was one of theirs. I'd stick him right now. I look straight into his eyes, my malice undisguised but I see no fear there. Just cold dead calm. Uncertainty digs at my brain. Have I really screwed up? Can't have. Thought outside the box. Put every ounce of my soul into it.

"HQ put me on the street. They chose the homeless beggar cover. It wasn't my call."

His mouth curls up at one side in an ugly half sneer of a smile.

"A beggar could have worked. Could've been invisible. But look at what you came up with. You had to be a dapper little tramp. You might have scuffed your shoes up a bit and dragged your suit through a hedge backwards but you're like a hobo in bloody Vogue. And don't try telling me that even rich people fall on hard times. Undercover means you're the rule, not the exception. And what's with the ridiculous limp and tea-towel wrapped around your foot? Please don't tell me you thought that was going to help you blend in. Oh for Christ's sake. Tell me that isn't what was going through your stupid head."

116

5.4 Succession

Title: Succession
Stimulus: Adventure of a coin, more broadly interpreted as a story where a coin is an important element.
Word count: 665

The deathly grey pallor of his mother's face assaulted Charles' eyes and the smell of death caused him to stifle a retch.

"Draw near me Charles."

Charles glanced towards Doctor Phipps who was irritably fiddling with his bag. Without looking up from whatever he was doing the doctor spoke.

"Only five minutes now. Remember, I am still Her Majesties physician and Her Royal Highness needs her rest."

Charles felt a nerve in his left eye start to twitch and angled that side of his face away from the doctor. Charles hated the man and if one thing was certain, when mother dear died, Doctor Phipps would be the first out of the door. Charles would make sure of that.

Despite her pain, the Queen immediately recognised her son's discomfort.

"Leave us now please doctor. I need a few words with my son."

As soon as the door closed behind the departing doctor the Queen spoke.

"You know that I never intended you to become King. I always hoped to skip a generation. It always pained me that you lacked a certain natural gravitas. But sadly, it looks like I am for this world now just a brief time and you will indeed have your way and succeed to the throne."

Charles ignored the slight, concentrating instead on his mother's last four words.

"Succeed to the throne. Yes. Thank you mother. I will do my utmost to maintain the honour and dignity of our family. But what is it that with me you so urgently need to speak?"

Irritated by Charles' pompous phrasing and lack of foresight the Queen snapped back despite her frailty. "Preparations for Succession must be made. You cannot sit at my heels until I'm buried. You must make preparations now."

"But mother. You may yet recover."

"Don't be silly Charles. One does not recover from death and without doubt I am surely dying. Now listen. This is of crucial importance. A realm cannot be without its currency and it is the living monarch that must assure their subjects of the value of their money. A promissory note from a dead person is worthless. Do you understand? It is your face that must now adorn each and every note and coin. The new money must be ready for immediate distribution upon my death."

Charles put his hand in his pocket and felt the round token concealed there. It was heavy and almost silky to the touch.

"But mother? Surely we can't discard all the circulating money?"

The Queen started to shake with anger.

"We? We? Are you totally without wit Charles? Not WE Charles. I'm not going to be here to hold your hand through this one. You'll need to stand up and make your own decisions. Of course you don't destroy the old currency. People will still use it. For a while they will even cherish it. But your face Charles, your face must appear on at least some of the circulated currency. By tradition the first circulation must be made on the very first working day following the day that I die. It is our duty to keep our promises to the people."

"Yes mother. I'll attend to it right away" said Charles, still fingering the small hard talisman that he had kept in his pocket for almost five years now.

Charles turned away from his mother and headed for the door. With his back turned to her he allowed himself a little smile. Without turning back to his mother he left the room and saw Doctor Phipps standing obediently by the door.

"Go back in doctor. I think you will find your patient somewhat more agitated than when you left."

As the doctor scurried back into the room Charles pulled the small heavy coin from his pocket. He smiled at the rich comforting gold and the effigy. The effigy was a likeness of himself and embossed in an arc over his crowned head were written the words, King Charles III.

5.5 See her now

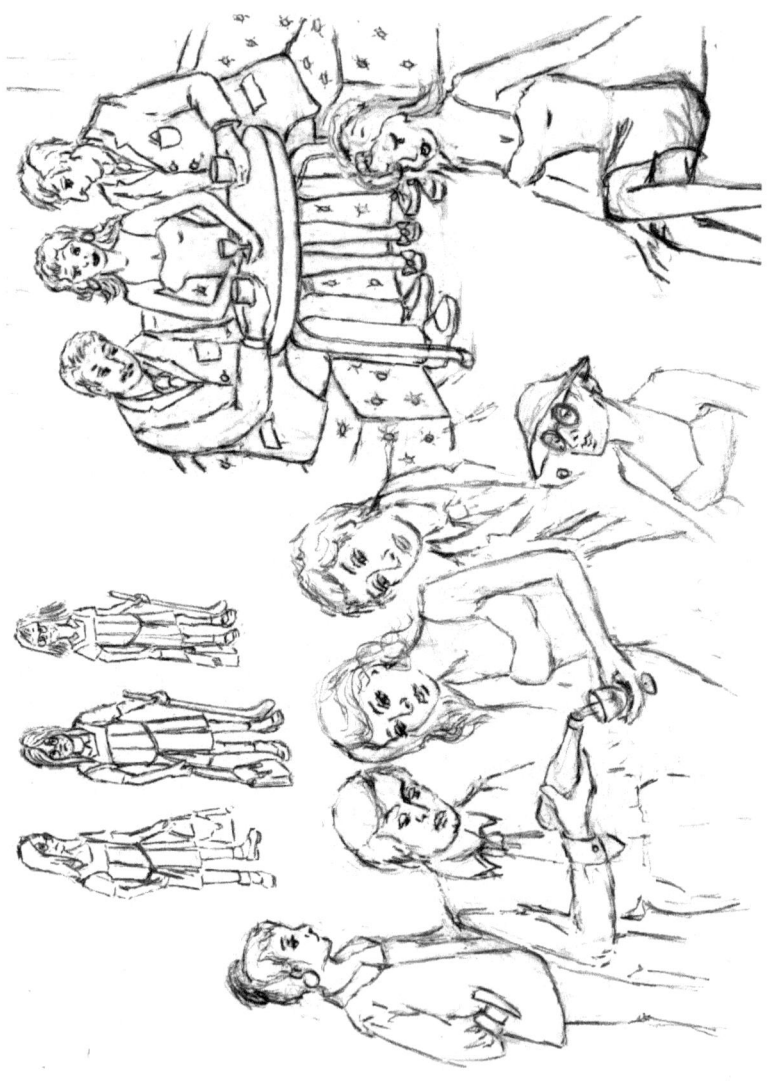

Title: See her now
Stimulus: money, cake, doll
Word count: 568

"Looking at her now you wouldn't believe what she used to be like."

My mate nods towards the booths along the dimly lit wall of the Pink Lady Hospitality Club. My head turns automatically to survey the area he's indicating.

I see a young woman with shoulder length tousled blonde hair squeezed between two middle-aged, overweight gentlemen in the end booth. I am immediately drawn to her. An irresistible attraction that grabs my eyes and holds them on her. She laughs and throws her head back enthusiastically. As she does so, her cleavage is accentuated by the low plunge of her meagre party dress which matches in colour the inviting glistening red of her lips. Even in the dim reddish glow which softly bathes the booth, it is impossible not to recognise her stunning looks and natural confident charm.

"Why? Who is she?"

"I used to go to school with her. Elizabeth Rowntree. That's her name. But she doesn't go by that now. Celestine. That's what they call her now. I reckon most of the kids we knew at school wouldn't recognise her now. But I do. You see, I saw her when she first started here. Not so confident then was she? Nope. A nervous wreck when she came in to audition as a hostess."

"So you were there at her audition."

"No, of course not. They hold the auditions in private out back but I recognised her right away when she came in. She loitered near the bar, looking extremely nervous I might add. She was like a fish out of water. I was just plucking up courage to go and talk to her when the Manager, Charlie Drake appears through the side door over there and leads her out back."

"She doesn't look like the nervous sort to me."

"Not now maybe, but at school. You should have seen her then. God she was pitiful. Full of spots. Always picking at them too. She used to walk around with her head bent forward so her face was hidden by her long hair. It was brown then. Long, lanky and greasy. She used to cake on this thick brown cream to try to disguise the acne but it made her look even worse. What a mess she was. She had a face only a mother could love and even a mother would struggle."

"I can't believe it. She's a total doll now."

"And she makes a fortune. You should see the money those blokes spend on her. And her tips, she makes more in one night than you make in a month."

"Are you sure she's the same girl?"

"Like I said, I was here when she came to audition. She wasn't blonde then. Still had her brown hair. She was different though. Her hair was really nice. Not greasy. And it was styled. No more spots either. I could see she was nervous, but even so, she still held her head high. I was shocked. She kind of looked the same, but then totally different at the same time. Even before the full transformation it was obvious she'd turned into a real looker. But then when she turned up the following night she'd suddenly become a blonde."

"Did you speak to her?"

"I was over like a shot. And we were getting on great too. That is, until she told me I had to pay."

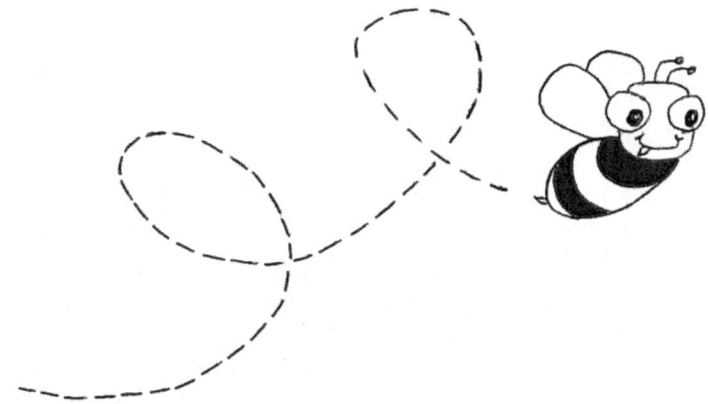

5.6 Garbage

Title: Garbage
Stimulus: memory stick, electronic tablet and mobile.
Word count: 1002

Beep.

I looked at the jumble of gadgets heaped around the room. The culprit lay in one of those heaps. Who could live in this mess? If Sam wasn't my brother I wouldn't even enter a room like this. Filthy pig. If only it was clean junk. God knows where he gets all this stuff. And the smell. Sweat and mould mixed with vomit and dog shit. Stop thinking about it. But it's too late and I stifle a retch. And this is where he's supposed to cook. Not that Sam was ever one for more than a slice of bread, not even buttered, sometimes with something wrapped in it as a poor substitute for a sandwich. Or a pre-cooked pie eaten unembellished direct from the plastic wrapper or cold beans eaten straight from the can.

Beep.

The sound was muffled but I managed to identify the direction. It was coming from the heap nearest the door.

"Sam. One of these God-damned things is beeping."

I don't know why I bother. Sam doesn't. I suppose his horde of rubbish is just another part of his illness. But one of those electronic things is still working. To describe the heaps of electrical junk as antique is an exaggeration but I'm still surprised that any of them has a working battery. Must be one of his newer acquisitions. Probably just an old fire alarm warning of a failing battery.

Beep.

It never ceases to amaze me how he loves things with wires but he never uses any of them. Part of his illness I suppose. Radio's, TV's, computers, electric toasters, old telephones, hair curlers, obsolete modems. He didn't buy the stuff. He raked it out of people's garbage. He just loves electrical things. Wires of every description. Spiral wires, straight wires, every gauge from speaker wire to cooker cable. There's even a short length that's armoured. It looks like Sam's been doing his best to restrain his soiled clothes, the way he has them wound around and trussed up in amongst the electrical junk. All these devices yet he never answers the telephone, he never turns on the cooker, he never even boils the kettle, seemingly content to drink his instant coffee made with unheated tap-water.

"How you getting on with the new medication?"

That's what I was really here to find out. The family want to know everything but they never soil themselves by paying Sam a visit.

Beep.

"It's an implant." Sam said as he came back into the kitchen and winced as he let himself down into a dining room chair that was only partly heaped with more of his treasure.

I watched him as he spoke but he didn't raise his head in my direction.

"The Doc described it as an electronic tablet. Says it releases hormones. Doesn't zonk me out like the pills used to. And I seem to remember things better. I'm not forgetting what I'm saying anymore."

"I thought you seemed much more on the ball than the last time I saw you. You haven't once had your memory stick mid-sentence and that's the first time in years. You're actually finishing your sentences without being distracted with other stuff going on inside your head. And you're not even stumbling around. You're a lot more mobile than before."

Beep.

"Confused and stumbling. So you know? You know how hard I find it to get about. Yet you never once thought to help me get to the hospital. Do you know it takes two buses to get there? Not once have any of you offered to take me. You all know I have to go for my monthly jabs."

Sam raised his head and looked at me for the first time since I arrived. Sam's stare was cold and angry. I don't trust him when he's agitated.

"But I didn't realise that you needed help getting there."

"I don't need help from you lot." Sam's eyes narrowed.

"I've just spent two weeks in hospital getting this thing stuck in me."

Sam twisted round and lifted the hair on the nape of his neck to show me the red remnants of a surgical cut running across a strange rectangular bulge concealed from casual view by his hair.

"That's my bloody battery pack. I'm like one of those toys. Whenever the batteries run out they have to open me up and put new ones in."

Beep.

"I thought you were just in as an out-patient."

I could feel my face flushing. Guilty, and I know it. Sam was getting more agitated by the second and I knew it was time to get out.

"But you never took the time to ask. Never bothered finding out. You only come around here so you can spread the gossip to the others. Not one of you even bothered to visit me in there."

It was true. That was exactly why I was there. I just hadn't ever really seen it like that.

"Look Sam, I'm sorry OK."

"Sorry, OK. Sorry, OK. No. No, it's not OK. And you're not sorry either. I might be crazy but I'm not stupid."

Tension was rising fast and I needed to deflate it. Sam's eyes looked totally crazed.

"You're not crazy Sam."

I felt insincere and prayed Sam didn't seem to notice.

"Don't talk like that. It's an illness, we all know that."

Beep.

"You better leave before you find out just how crazy I am. Go on. Get out. You bloody hypocrite. Coming around here like you care. Get out."

I knew better than to stick around. As teenagers I had seen Sam lose it and I knew that I was winding him up just by being there.

"Right Sam, I'm going to get off then."

"Too damn right you're getting off. Go on. Get out."

Beep.

I left without another word. I climbed into my car but made no attempt to start it. I was suddenly overwhelmed. He was right. We were all bloody hypocrites.

5.7 Did it really matter?

Title: Did it really matter?
Stimulus: In the end, it didn't matter.
Word count: 841

"In the end, it didn't matter did it?" said Karen in a menacing tone.

"You still slept with her didn't you? Well, didn't you?"

Karen's eyes were pure venom, her lips a vicious snarl. Even now, when Karen was at her most vile, she was beautiful. Beautiful, yes, but not my Karen. Her beauty was tarnished. Ugly. She disgusted me. How could my little angel be so repulsive.

I swallowed my hurt and worked hard to bury the feelings I couldn't bear to face. The anger. The desperate fear. I drew on every reserve to speak evenly but couldn't quite manage to disguise my emotion.

"I didn't. I never slept with anyone. I certainly didn't sleep with Sarah. Do you really think I would sleep with her? No. You can't blame me for breaking up this family. It's you who wants to leave. You just can't find it in you to give it a real try. You're making things up to excuse what you're doing. Deserting us. Deserting our children. Desert me if you want but Lucy and Katie? How can you leave them?"

My head shook in disbelief.

"How could you?"

It hardly seemed possible but her face hardened even further. I don't know if I took a step back but I felt myself physically recoil. There was only hatred.

"I don't know what I ever saw in you. Call yourself a man? I don't even care what you did with Sarah. In fact I believe you. You haven't got the balls to have an affair."

"Nothing ever happened between me and Sarah. She's just a friend. That's all. Something you wouldn't understand. Friendship. You don't know what friendship is."

Karen looked with pure hatred.

"That's right. Talk, talk, talk. That's you all over. Probably talking about me. 'Ne, ne, ne, she's so horrid to me, whine, whine, whine, she's so nasty, ne, ne, ne.' You make me sick. Like you think talking about me to fat, ugly Sarah isn't being unfaithful. You disgust me."

I was shocked at how much she hated me. As if I had murdered a child. Or worse. As if I had murdered our children. But it wasn't me who was the killer. It was her. She was killing our family. She was ripping out my heart. Breaking us. She had changed. A monster. She had become a monster.

Even though I knew there was no love left in her. No love for me. No love for our family. I couldn't help myself. I couldn't stop myself from pleading. I couldn't stop myself begging.

"Karen. Please. Just take a moment to really think about what you are doing. Please. You have to change your mind. For the girls. If not for me, for the girls. They need their mother. They need you Karen."

My pleading only inflamed her more.

"Blackmail. Using the girls. That's about your level. Hiding behind our daughters. That's pathetic. In fact you're pathetic. Stop you're damned snivelling. It's sickening. And anyway, it's over. We're finished. And, as a matter of fact, it's all your fault. If you had been a real man, someone I could respect? But looking at you now I can't imagine what possessed me to marry you in the first place. It doesn't matter what you say, I'm leaving, and that's final."

I couldn't hold the emotion. Anger and pain exploded from me.

"It doesn't matter? It doesn't matter? How can you say that? You bitch. You nasty bitch."

Karen smiled.

"That's right. I am a nasty bitch. And thanks. Calling me a bitch just makes it all the easier to leave. Try thinking about that when you're on your own at night."

She started laughing and swept up her bag as she turned to leave. I wanted to run at her. I wanted to smash her in the back of the head. I wanted to beat her, and beat her, and beat her. But I just stood there and watched her walk out. She left the door swinging open. A final antagonising message to tell me that she didn't care. Worse, to tell me that she hated me.

I slammed my fist into the wall, crying out as the searing pain shot through my wrist and up my arm. I looked to see if she heard my cry but all I saw was her back, striding away down the path. She didn't even turn her head.

I shouted after her, "Of course it matters," but my words sounded empty, hollow, almost without meaning.

"It does matter. It does matter." I wanted it to matter. I needed it to matter. It did matter. It mattered to me.

"It does matter" I shouted again.

I collapsed to my knees. Tears flooded from my eyes. And in my mind the realisation I couldn't bear to face. The realisation that she had changed. Karen didn't care. Hurting me didn't matter. Leaving Lucy and Katie didn't matter. Our family? Finally I understood. To Karen, in the end, none of us mattered.

5.8 Integrity

Title: Integrity
Stimulus: Scene development for a larger work.
Word count: 1172

"That boy's got no integrity. My only son and he behaves like this."

Dad waved a crumpled piece of paper at me as if in explanation. His voice was argumentative and angry but behind the anger his eyes showed a deep sorrow. Something had upset him and upset him bad. I had a good idea of what was written on the note he was brandishing at me but there was no way I was going to let on. He looked at the paper again, straightening it with a stroking caress so at odds with the anger in his voice. As he did so, I was able to see that it was actually quite a long letter, carefully scripted in neat straight lines despite the un-ruled paper. It was Tom's writing alright. Dad suddenly glared at me. I was affronted but said nothing. I knew Dad too well to speak. Better to just let him spit it out himself.

"If only Mathew had lived. He would've been ...., well, he wouldn't have been like Tom anyway. This, this ...."

Dad shook the letter at me again.

"This is an insult to your mother's memory. How could he be so cowardly. A damned note. A damned note to tell us what he has done. And it's an insult to you as well. Didn't have the decency to even tell his own sister he was leaving."

Dad's eyes narrowed accusingly.

"You didn't. Did you know? Did you? Were you in on it? Were you? What did he tell you? Come on. What did he say to you?"

I wasn't going to be fooled into speaking but my stomach knotted at the accuracy of his accusation. I silently begged, who I was not sure, myself? God? I was begging someone to help me not to betray myself. Begging against own guilt. I cringed at the insult to God but still I remained silent. Seconds seemed like minutes whilst he searched my eyes for answers. I hardly dared breathe. Blood rose to flush my cheeks. Had I betrayed myself? Could he see the complicity written in the red of my face?

At last he broke the silent fury.

"No, of course you didn't know ... Its Tom ... He's left."

I knew now that I was expected to speak. He expected me to ask what had happened. It was required. And in asking my innocence would be implied. In fact more than implied. My innocence would be proven. There was no need to tell him that I already knew that Tom was going to leave. No need to explain that Tom had sworn me to secrecy. No need to make Dad feel that I had betrayed him. Betrayed him by choosing my promise of secrecy to Tom over my duty of disclosure to my father. Why should I hurt him any more than he was already hurt? I couldn't tell him a direct lie. Well, I suppose I could directly lie but that was the very last thing that I wanted to do. As long as my innocence existed in his mind then the hurt would not be doubled.

"What has happened Dad? What does the letter say?"

"He's left. Tom has left. Didn't have the balls to look me in the eye and tell me. Took the coward's way out. Well I can tell you, he's no damned son of mine. He never did have any balls. Never did have any backbone. No integrity. That's Tom. Absolutely no integrity."

I tried to make sense of the words but struggled. I thought that I knew what integrity was but suddenly realised that I didn't really. I tried to work out what exactly it was that Tom lacked, what was the omission from Tom's character that riled Dad so much. Embroiled in the tension of the situation my mind flailed for meaning but it was impossible to formulate any real definition. All I knew was that it was bad and not the sort of thing that I would want my Dad to think of me. I spoke softly, only semi-conscious of the fact that I was desperate to placate my father's anger with the gentleness of my tone.

"Tom wouldn't mean any harm, I'm sure."

"Not mean it? That's exactly the point. He tries to play at Honest John, all those words. Trying to imply he's a decent

138

human being. A man of his word. But he's not a man. There is no man in Tom. No man at all. His words are meaningless. He doesn't even know what he thinks. He hasn't a single ounce of moral courage. He can make a show of being honest. Yes, he can do that alright. And he had me fooled. Had us all fooled. But look at this."

Dad waved the paper at me once more.

"He knew I was against him moving in with that damned girl. Looks like that idiot boy has now got her pregnant. But he couldn't face the music. Not Tom. No. Tom has to scurry away like the pathetic little mouse he is. Couldn't face me. Weak. Weak and pathetic. It saddens me that I ever spawned such a coward. He knows he's wrong. As soon as he has to stand up for his own behaviour, this is what he does. Absolutely no integrity. I don't know how he thinks they're going to survive? How is he going to look after her? And a bloody baby? When he can't even face his own father. How does he think he's going to face up to life without being able to own up to what he does. That's the real disappointment."

Dad's face softened and I suddenly noticed that his eyes were wet. He never cried. At least, I had never seen him cry. But the mix of anger, frustration and sorrow were showing.

"Integrity. That's Tom's problem. Integration between actions and belief. It's at the core of our moral fibre. Without that we're nothing."

Dad looked directly into my eyes and stretched his hands out towards me.

"Come here. Come here sweetheart."

I moved towards him obediently and allowed him to collect me into his embrace. His arms wrapped around me and pulled me to him, my cheek on his chest, the musty safe smell, the softness of his cotton shirt. Warm and safe. My arms dangled limply by my side. It was rare and because of that there was a slight awkwardness. But instinctively I knew he loved me deep down. I felt the rumble of his voice through the wall of his chest.

"Don't you be weak. For God's sake sweetheart, don't be like Tom. At least I have you. My brave little girl. At least I have you."

Once more guilt flushed me. My whole being sank with the knowledge of what was in my heart. He didn't have me. I wasn't staying. I was going to leave just like Tom. And, just like Tom, I didn't have the integrity to tell him.

5.9 No win, no fee

Title: No win, no fee
Stimulus: Lawyer
Word count: 135

You're angry. The news isn't good. You didn't even want to make a personal injury claim. If that bloody lawyer hadn't convinced you that it was the right thing to do.

"Leave yourself wide open if you don't." That's what he said. "Protects you from a counter claim."

Well that's exactly what you've got. In fact, the other guy said that he only made the counter claim because you claimed first. You bloody fool. Listen to lawyers will you? Don't you know they're in it for themselves. And now you have a case to defend.

"No win, no fee", he said. "You can't lose."

Then you end up being sued. And then what does the lawyer say to you?

He says, "I'm afraid defending against a counter claim, well that's a whole different ball game."

Write with Flash Companion

The Write with Flash Companion is a collection of short works that complement this book. For further details visit:

Ampurlife.com

List of books by Stephen Mark Richards

A brief synopsis for each book follows this list.

Tornado Spring

This is the true story of a journey through the full height of the United States during the worst tornado outbreak on record.

Wild Summer

We travelled west through the Rocky Mountains to the Pacific Ocean, up through Canada's Cascade Mountains and then south, through the giant coastal redwood forests, to San Francisco.

Desert Winter

It is an adventure of a life-time, from the Pacific to the Atlantic, traversing the deserts of the southern United States.

Conquering America

The trilogy of Tornado Spring, Wild Summer and Desert Winter in one complete volume.

Florida without Disney

How can a visitor to Florida embark on an amazing journey through time and space?

Write with Flash

Discover the secrets of storytelling and perhaps you will soon be sharing your unique story.

Short Shorts and Shorts: Volume 1

The first volume in a series of short story books fully illustrated by Joyce. Unsuitable for young children.

Holly Marie and the Small Tall Tree

Holly Marie explored the world of observation with her friend Rabbit. For children 2 to 6 years.

Tornado Spring

The average number of tornados in the USA for the month of April is normally around 135 but in April 2011 there were over 600. It was the worst month for tornados in United States records. On April 27th there were over 190 tornados recorded, the most ever in a single day. The tornado outbreak of April 2011 killed over 350 people, 65 in Tuscaloosa, Alabama on April 27th alone. This was the deadliest tornado outbreak in over 85 years. It was at the beginning of April 2011 that we embarked on our journey with the aim of driving a motorhome around the USA. We planned to complete the tour in three stages the first of which would take us from Florida in the south up the eastern side of America to the Canadian border. We were not to know that we would be travelling the full height of the United States during the worst tornado outbreak on record. This is the true story of that journey.

Wild Summer

"it don't get any more real"

stephen mark
RICHARDS

Wild Summer

Of course adventure is for the rich and famous but it is also for ordinary people too. Anniversaries or even a New Year resolution will suffice to focus the mind and help to make things happen. Any year is a good year for an adventure and any excuse is a good excuse too. All we need is the inspiration, the determination and the desire. This book tells the story of the second stage of our around North America journey. On this journey, the second of three stages, we travelled from Chicago to San Francisco, visiting the Yellowstone super-volcano and encountering bears, elk, moose and whales along the way. We travelled west through the Rocky Mountains to the Pacific Ocean up through Canada's Cascade Mountains and then south, through the giant coastal redwood forests, to San Francisco. Wild Summer tells the trials and tribulations of that voyage.

Desert Winter

Desert Winter takes us on an adventure of a life-time, from the Pacific to the Atlantic, traversing the southern United States. The journey leads us through mountains, giant redwood forests, and deserts to large cities, natural wonders, national treasures and even alien encounters. It carries us to the edge of the precipice, within swiping distance of bears claws and striking range of a rattlesnakes fangs. Wandering streets from urban wonders to urban dereliction we gain insights into American culture from the perspective of an outsider. Vicariously revel in the adventure or grasp the encouragement to travel - the choice yours.

Conquering America

Explore the United States from a unique perspective as you are taken on a journey of excitement and adventure. Experience American cultures and natural treasures as never before on a roller-coaster trip from sadness and fear to joy and wonder. By the time you reach the end you will be eager to do it all again but this time you will surely be the traveller yourself.

This book was prompted by the successful completion of an epic journey around America and the publication of three books: Tornado Spring; Wild Summer and Desert Winter which document the author's adventures. Conquering America brings together these three books to present, for the first time, the entire adventure in a single volume

Florida without Disney

Florida without Disney shows how you can take your own
personal visit to Florida, or anywhere else for that matter, and
use it to link yourself to an entire universe of knowledge,
understanding and adventure. People of all ages, children and
adults alike, are stimulated by: facts stranger than fiction;
surprising revelations; truelife adventures; close encounters in the
wild; and cultures in all their incredible variety. Florida without
Disney brings all these elements together in a book
encompassing time from prehistory to the present along with
locations from around the world and beyond. It provides a
template for injecting greater fascination, interest and curiosity
into your own journeys through life.

Write with Flash

Flash is a writing form that can help aspiring writers transform their ideas into completed works and Write with Flash aims to show how that can be achieved. Many people have written books but their number pales into insignificance when compared to the number of people who would like to write a book but never do. This does not mean that those unwritten books would have been without merit. On the contrary, what it really means is that millions of fascinating stories go to the grave with their would-be creators. The sad fact is, the unique qualities that each of those potential creators would have brought to those untold stories were never shared.

Short Shorts and Shorts: Volume 1

This book is unsuitable for young children as it does contain some violent scenes and some limited use of profanities in the context of creating authentic language. Here are the opening lines of the first two stories.

'All the young people, children and teenagers, all that is except for me, loved that time of year, the third week in September, when Joe Sowerby's Circus came to town.'

'When Shirley Stokes, an attractive young mother, moved into number 4 with her new baby everyone was overjoyed. Everyone that is, except for Kay Powell.'

Holly Marie and the Small Tall Tree

Observation is the basis of knowledge in both the arts and the sciences. We are not born with all the tools and formal skills required to make sense of the world but rather, we develop these skills over time. For over 50 years, psychologists have known that these skills develop in stages during childhood but until now there has been little in the way of book-based education to support this crucial aspect of child development. At last, in Holly Marie, we have the tools to enable our children to develop their understanding of the world. For children 2 to 6 years.

Ampurlife Books

Find these and other books by Stephen Mark Richards at:

Ampurlife.com

If you have any comments or would like to leave a review then please do so on Amazon
You can also contact us directly on:

Ampurlife@gmail.com